The Ultimate Guide to Traveling More and Spending Less

Russell Hannon

BTTB

Published in Canada by Break the Travel Barrier

Break the Travel Barrier is a trademark and the floating island colophon is a registered trademark of Break the Travel Barrier, Inc.

Break the Travel Barrier books are available at special discounts for bulk purchases for sales promotions and commercial use. Special editions, including personalized covers, excerpts of existing books, or books with corporate logos can be accommodated. Submit requests via e-mail to: info@breakthetravelbarrier.com.

Stop dreaming… start traveling: the ultimate guide to traveling more and spending less / by Russell Hannon

ISBN 978-0-9947584-0-8

Printed in the United States of America

Book Design by RED DOOR MEDIA
www.reddoormediadesign.com

First Edition

PRAISE FOR

Stop Dreaming…
Start Traveling

"This book is the ultimate Get Out Of Town FREE card! It is chock full of tips, tricks, steals and deals. Russell quiets any doubts about being able to travel more often, to better destinations, on less money without skimping on luxury. Get this book and pack your bags. You're in for a whole new adventure!"

–**DANETTE KUBANDA**, Emmy Winning TV Producer, Publicity Consultant, Media Coach, Writer, 2011/2012 "Woman of the Year"– National Association of Professional Women. danettekubanda.com

"This is more than a travel book, it's a life training book that defies the cliché "You get what you pay for." Readers will realize the pleasure that can come from intelligently maximizing the value of their travel dollar. This book will change your travel destiny."

–**ARTHUR VON WIESENBERGER**, Host of *Around The World Travel TV*

"Inexpensive travel doesn't need to be no frills. Russell has done the research and brings together tips and resources to maximize your travel dollar while doing it in style!"

–**SIMON DONATO**, PhD, Star of *Boundless TV* and founder of *Adventure Science*

"Russell makes it easy for you to save time and money by pulling together great travel tips and resources into this concise quick reference manual."

–**PATRICK SOJKA**, Founder of Rewardscanada.ca and frequentflyerbonuses.com

"I wish I had this book years ago. Russell covers every angle from planning and budgeting to short-cuts, cost-saving advice and overall safety. It's a required reading for anyone looking to get more value for their travel dollar. Don't plan another trip until you read this book!"

–**ROD MORGAN**, President, Sigma Plus Solutions Inc., Lean Six Sigma Quality Consulting

"This book has the greatest ways to save money while traveling. It covers all aspects of travel from A-Z and I gladly recommend it."

–**TRAVEL COACH CHRIS**, President, Lifetime Leisure Experiences

To all who have inspired me along the way, those who walk with me today, and those whose path I've yet to cross

and

to Robbie McHugh,

who always laughed loudly at how I pulled off so many free trips. His enthusiasm triggered an insane moment of clarity during a 5 a.m. taxi ride to the airport on a frigid February morning in 2012. That was the moment I first envisioned sharing my journey in these pages. I wish you were here so that I could share it with you. This one's for you, #1.

Disclaimer

If you are looking to wind down with a bedtime read, you're about to ruin your chances of sleeping soundly. Readers have been known to experience:

- A sharp spike in exhilarating travel experiences–without the bill
- Hair-raising goose bumps
- A rush to finish the book in one sitting
- Ceaseless ranting about what they've learned about how to save money traveling

Contents

First Things First

Part I – Yours for the Taking

Part II – Build Your Dream Travel Plan

Part III – Live It, Love It

First Things First

FAQ

WHAT'S IN IT FOR ME?

In a world flooded with travel literature that tells you where to go and what to do, here are answers to some questions you may ask before deciding whether to read on:

Can this book this really help me?

This book can help everyone who has felt the sting of a post-holiday credit card bill or thinks they need to postpone that trip until they save more. If you're sick of paying the going rate and are looking to find ways to get around it, this book will change your travel destiny.

How much can I save?

If every American used just one tip from this book to save $200 on his or her next trip, $64 billion would be redirected from airlines into travelers' pockets. And that hardly scratches the surface because you are going to save a lot more than $200, $2,000, or $12,000. When you do the math—especially taking into account some dramatic savings—this book could trigger the greatest liberation in travel since the start of commercial aviation and permanently change the dynamics of the travel industry.

Does it involve much work?

No. In fact, you will get immediate results by simply planning better and thinking differently. The advanced and complex strategies are laid out step-by-step, making them easy to apply.

Do I have to radically change my life?

Nyet. The strategies in this book are simple enough to apply to any trip or lifestyle. Everything isn't for everyone, but everyone will find dozens of tips, tools, and strategies that will work for them.

Do I have to be young, free-spirited, and single?

Nein. Whether you're a business traveler, student, retiree, or you have a family, you will learn practical ways to fund your travels. You might be interested in traveling for a cause, participating in events, or getting free travel by organizing group trips. Maybe you want to start a travel-writing business to offset your costs. No matter what you want, all the information you need is right here.

What if I can already afford to travel?

Those who have the most money are at the highest risk of leaving too much on the table. Not only will you save money, you will have fun doing it and will want to brag about how you're saving it.

Must I live like a pauper?

Au contraire. You can travel on your own terms for what it costs to stay home and watch travel shows, without compromising your lifestyle.

Why You Need This Book...

You may not realize it yet, but by purchasing this book, you have gotten the deal of a lifetime. Just use a few tricks from this book once, and you'll get travel savings worth more than *ten times* the cost of the book. But that's just the beginning; you will be able to travel five times more on the same budget, pull off a handful of free trips each year, and cut *five figures* off your future travel costs. Forget winning the lottery, and forget waiting until next year: Whether you're a five-star traveler, a hitchhiking backpacker, or anyone in between, you can travel the world for less than it costs to stay home and be an armchair traveler—with a handful of free trips thrown in to boot!

If you don't believe me, keep reading and give me a chance to prove you wrong. My mission is to empower you to travel wherever, however, and as much as you want. This book is literally your passport to the world, and I'm so confident it will dramatically change your travel lifestyle that on the last page I'll invite you to share your opinions online with fellow readers and travelers. You'll be able to say anything about this book, including what you learned, how you used it, and how much you saved.

What You Need to Know

You are throwing your money away! From surcharges to tourist traps, you are constantly being assaulted with deceivingly low posted rates that are tied to hidden surcharges, fees, and strict policies that add up to billions of dollars paid by travelers every year.

The big fad in executive boardrooms is to charge as much as customers are willing to pay, rather than what services are really worth. That's why hotel and airfare prices bounce up and down like yo-yos. It's also what makes travel seem expensive.

Your last vacation likely cost you *five* times more than it needed to. Just imagine paying Ritz-Carlton prices to live at home every day.

Why should you have to pay more to eat, sleep, surf the web, and use your phone than the locals next to you pay for the same things? It's outrageous, but it's only half of the problem. The other half is that, once you finally do break loose and take that trip you spent *all* year anticipating, your travel-starved soul gladly pays the going rate in the name of not depriving yourself over a few dollars. I call this "budget amnesia." It's the reason millions of travelers pay too much every day for too little and cannot afford to travel more than they do. Although this happens to the savviest of travelers, the reality is that you don't have to spend those dollars.

"But I Can Already Afford to Travel"

It doesn't matter if you can afford to sail your life away on a yacht; that doesn't mean that you should pay the asking price to do it! There is a saying that goes, "A fool and his money are soon parted," and those who have an abundance of money are most likely to squander it. If the game was to spend all of our money, these would be the winners:

- **Theoren Fleury**: This former NHL star and Olympic gold medalist gets the bronze this time for his article on "How to Blow $50 Million."
- **Nicolas Cage**: Our silver medalist blew $150 million on a jet, fleets of yachts and Rolls Royce's, a dozen mansions, and enough art to stock a museum.
- **Mike Tyson**: Our undisputed champ found a way to plough through $400 million.

Chasing an image or "nice to haves" will put you in the poorhouse and keep you there. The richest person in the room is far more frugal than you would expect. Just look at Warren Buffett: One of the world's richest men owns a private jet company but still flies commercially because it's hundreds of times cheaper. The point is you should be proud of your money-saving exploits and your ability to get more for much less than what everyone else pays.

Why Travel Matters

"Carpe diem. Seize the day boys, make your lives extraordinary!"
– Robin Williams, *Dead Poet's Society*

In the end, ultra-economical travel is not about saving a dollar for its own sake. It's about not letting the going rate of travel keep you from being where you need to be or from living out priceless experiences. For some, it's about the spouse they met while island hopping. For others, it's about the lifelong friends they made along the way. For many, it's about the thrill of a lifetime they'll never forget.

But it's also about much more than that. It's about someone I know who missed her father's funeral because she could not afford to fly home. It's about how much more tolerant the world would be if every child had more exposure to different cultures. It's also about your health. Stress eventually kills, which is why breaking away from your routine is as important to your health as dieting, exercise and sleeping well.

I'd like to share a story that made me realize why ultra-economical travel is as important as having an emergency savings and a nest egg for retirement. It started when I got an e-mail from Rob, a close college friend who was sharing his excitement about a tour he was planning. He wanted to catch a dozen football games across the country including the Rose Bowl, LSU vs. Alabama, Florida vs. Florida State, a Monday night game in Seattle, and the list went on …

Rob invited me to meet up with him at any of these games, but he highlighted one specific game in Green Bay that six of our college buddies were also attending. My first reaction was, "Green Bay in December? Why not Dallas, San Diego, or Tampa?" My second thought was, "I'm just so busy." I planned my schedule six months out and figured there would be other opportunities to get together down the road. So I replied, "Rob, I just don't think I can make it this year. But don't give up on me, we'll make it to a game one day."

I got busy with life again, but every once in a while I stopped and thought, "It really would be nice to see all the guys again. With everyone scattered across the continent, how often will we have the chance to be together at the same time?"

Fast forward to Saturday, December 7th, 2013: As I readied for bed in a Philadelphia hotel room, I saw a Facebook post from the guys clowning around in Green Bay, and I joined in on the conversation:

Russell Hannon Hey I'll be in the neighborhood tomorrow. You guys mind if I crash your party?
December 7, 2013 at 9:04pm · Like · 1

The following morning, my flight home connected through Chicago O'Hare Airport. I called the airline and paid a $90 change fee to delay the second leg of my flight by two days so that I could catch the game.

As I walked into the stadium and descended toward Lambeau Field, I was as frozen as the tundra, but it was all fine. Our seats were ten rows from the field, and the Packers had just scored. The place was rocking and, as I looked down, for the first time in 13 years, I saw the guys all together. They were giving each other high-fives, laughing, and taking pictures. They glanced up, saw me coming towards them, and erupted "Rusty!" in a burst of happy cheers. I felt this huge wave of happiness.

That day was priceless. Even more so because, three months later, I received a private Facebook message late one night saying, "It's about Rob … call me." Rob had passed away. In the incredibly depressing days that followed, I felt almost ashamed that I had turned down so many chances to see him and that I almost passed on the Green Bay game as well.

That's when it hit me, *"This is why travel matters."* We need to be ultra-economical travelers so that we don't one day have to live with the regret of having missed an important life event due to the cost of getting there, only to later realize that we could have gone for a fraction of the going rate.

What Price Freedom?

How much should the adventure of a lifetime cost? Can you put a dollar value on lifelong international friendships? You don't need a calculator; you probably already know the answer. There is absolutely no link between what you spend and having the thrill of a lifetime. That's because excitement isn't measured in dollars and cents. In fact, having the time of your life doesn't have to cost anything. But the great irony is that, even though travel experiences are priceless, cost is the biggest barrier that keeps millions from traveling.

Time Is Money

We all know someone who drives to the other end of town to save $4 to fill their gas tank. At what point does the effort to save a dollar no longer justify the effort to save it? It really depends. The wealthier you are, the less time you are willing to spend to save a buck. On the other hand, if you are cash poor, you will search far and wide to save a small sum.

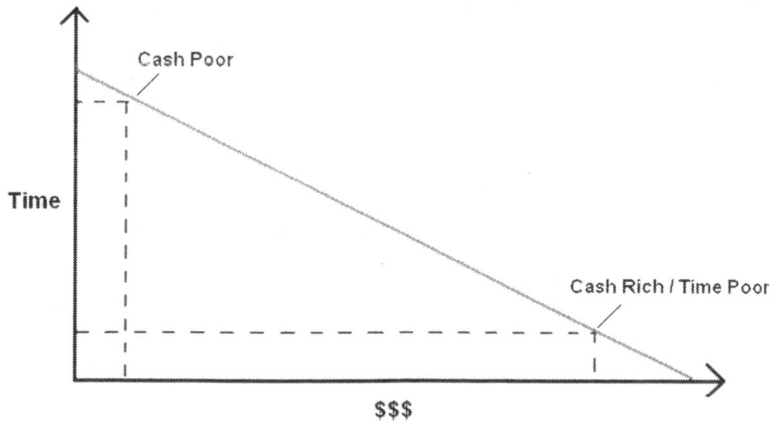

One secret to traveling more on the same budget is to break away from this tendency and act cash poor regardless of where you fall on the scale. People who stay rich and those who get by on very little have one thing in common: Every day they wage a war against a world that tries to take their money from them, and they refuse to pay more than they absolutely need to. Although you may not realize it, you are also waging this war. Whether you choose to fight back or not will determine whether you get ahead or fall behind.

Three Things Keep Us from Traveling the World Over

1. Dollars and Cents

Most travelers spend five times more than they need to because the travel industry charges, on average, five times the local cost of living. The average three-star hotel room goes for $150 a night. Compare that to the cost of a one-bedroom apartment down the street that rents for $900 a month. That's only $30 a night. The same applies for restaurants; eating out three times a day will cost you five times more than your average grocery bill. All the while, bills back home keep coming in. This is insane! More so, it baffles me that most people are brainwashed by the idea that this is what they *have* to pay to travel.

2. The World Caters to Locals ...

The system we live under was designed for the world as it was 100 years ago. We are land-locked to one place because of our mortgages, which keep us from straying away for too long. The dream of using remote connectivity to work from a cabana in Tahiti has fizzled into a leash that keeps us connected to the office while on vacation.

When we finally do travel, we pay more than locals for the same goods and services. That's because the travel industry knows travelers aren't rational with their money so businesses inflate their prices, knowing travelers will pay the asking price. All the while, locals get discounts from vendors who hope for repeat business.

3. The World Is Also a Couple's World ...

Advertised deals are rarely what they appear to be. Travel operators tease you with enticing rates, which usually include fine print that assumes double occupancy and charges solo travelers single supplement surcharges. Every day, I find a handful of deceiving "deals" tagged to fine print such as:

"Per night per person, assumes double occupancy"

"Non-refundable, no changes allowed"

"Valid Sunday through Thursday except on statutory holidays"

"Available for dine-in only from 1 – 4 p.m."

You do have a choice. You can put this book down and accept the system as it is, along with the restrictions that will clip your travel wings. Or, you can continue reading and pave your own path with unique strategies to turbocharge your travel IQ. After reading this book, you will be a twenty-first century travel expert with the ability to go anywhere for a lot less than you ever thought possible.

Why Listen to Me?

First I yelled, then I begged, and finally I cried ...

"Isn't there anything you can do for me?" I pleaded to the customer service agent, as it sunk in that I was going to have to pony up $2,108 for a cell phone bill that I racked up in just two weeks abroad.

That was ten years ago, and I was hardly a travel expert back then. I thought I had to settle for one big trip each year. I spent months saving up for one trip and often spent a few more paying the balance. Although I did my best to find the best fares, hotels were still expensive (even when cramping four people to a room). The little bit I saved from taking 6 a.m. flights was nominal, and that $2,108 cell phone bill was the breaking point. I had been beaten into believing that travel was inherently expensive.

The great irony was that my day job as a lean management professional was to find ways to improve results in less time using less money. Lean management is traditionally used to improve manufacturing, production, and administrative processes, but I said to myself, "There has to be a way I can apply lean principles to travel more and spend less." Fast forward ten years and lean management is the backbone of what I call ultra-economical travel. It's how I pulled off a dozen free trips and visited many of the world's most expensive cities, like London, Monaco, Tokyo and New York, for less than my at-home cost of living.

Unlike most travel advice that is subject-specific and tells you where to go and what to do, the principles in this book are timeless and universal. They are what separates this book from all of the other travel advice out there. Thank goodness I found my way to the other side: Now, I'm going to show you how to join me.

Excuses be Gone

"The most dangerous risk of all – the risk of spending your life not doing what you want on the bet you can buy yourself the freedom to do it later."

– Randy Komisar, *The Monk and the Riddle*

We all have the same excuses:

"I have no one to travel with."

"I don't have enough time or vacation."

"I can't afford it."

"When I retire …"

"When the kids grow up …"

Too many people say they would have made it to Disney World, if only … Whatever your Disney World is, there will always be a reason to not go. If you wait for the stars to line up, chances are you will never achieve your travel dreams. The world is filled with opportunities that can change your life, but they will only come to fruition if you step up to the plate and swing!

What This Book Is

In this age of easy credit, anyone can hop on a plane and live large for a few weeks. But having a travel lifestyle is a whole different ballgame. If you want to travel more frequently without feeling the pinch, you either need to:

Make a lot more money,

Spend a lot less, or

Both.

Using this book, you won't need to make more money, skimp on lifestyle, sell your home, or leave your life. You don't need to hitch-hike or stay in dodgy motels (but you certainly can, if you want to). I have never hitchhiked. I stay in fully furnished apartments, enjoy great restaurants, and indulge in the comforts of luxury. I travel often, in style, and I don't need a trust fund to afford it, nor do I need to quit my job. Keep reading, and soon you will be saying the same.

You Get What You Give

What you ultimately get out of this book depends on how much you use it. If you use this book to its full potential, you can literally squeeze water out of a stone to save hundreds (if not thousands) of dollars on every trip you take. Over the course of a lifetime, that adds up to five figures easily.

Myth: "It isn't possible to travel free."

Every day, someone tells me that it isn't realistic to travel for free. First, free travel doesn't mean doing it without spending a penny. It's doing it without adding to your everyday cost of living and not spending more than what you would have, had you stayed home and kept to your daily routine.

As long as you keep your costs of food and transportation on par with your at-home budget, these expenses are not costing you anything to travel; you would be incurring them at home, anyway.

Even though hotels are as expensive as they have ever been, and you cannot put your mortgage or rent payments on hold while traveling, there have never been more alternatives for free and inexpensive accommodations. As for discretionary travel expenses, such as roaming fees, checked bags, currency conversion charges, or ATM fees, know that if a local doesn't have to pay it, there's a way to get around it.

My Great Revelation

"You're saying that I could have gone to Daytona Beach for free!?"

Three months prior to making this revelation, I never would have imagined that it was possible. It all started the day a captain on my college football team approached me and said, "I'm organizing a spring break trip to Daytona Beach, and I want you to be there with us. The weather will be great, the beaches will be packed, and you are going to have the time of your life. Here's the deal, $450 will cover your transportation and accommodations for a week, and you will share a room with three teammates."

With all my teenage exuberance, I responded, "I'm in!" So I called Mom and Dad asking for $450, and I'll just they weren't as enthusiastic about it as I was. The guys did such a great job promoting the trip that they packed two buses, and I felt deflated as I watched them pull away because I wasn't on either of them. I spent the week playing video games. Imagine my surprise when someone mentioned that the guys who organized the trip couldn't afford to go either! But they went for free because they each found ten people to sign up for the trip at the going rate. They did this by running a campaign where they put posters up all over campus and bought the DJ at the campus pub drinks to plug the trip for them. "Hmmm ... had I known about this, I could be at Daytona Beach." As I looked out the window at the snow falling, I thought, "That's a clever way to get around the system. I wonder what other ways there are to get around the system?"

This is the book that is going to teach you how to get around the system. Now buckle up because you're in for a trip of a lifetime.

What Makes This Book Unique?

"It takes a lot of hard work to make something simple, to truly understand the challenges and come up with elegant solutions."

– Steve Jobs

You probably already have a few clever ways to save money while traveling. Maybe you have a favorite website or learned a few tricks along the way. When you think about how much you've saved with what you know, imagine how much more you could save if you had a pipeline feeding you the very best deals for you to cherry pick. This book is different from all the other travel advice out there in that it goes one step further, leveraging all of the following into one system to multiply your savings:

- Loopholes
- Timeless models
- Proven repeatable systems
- The best websites
- Credit card travel benefits

- Loyalty programs
- Key factors that play a hand in any travel deal
- Proven strategies to overcome the financial barriers to travel
- Ways to find and capture the best deals for you
- Practical ways to pull off free trips

This system shows you how to build and live out your custom-tailored **Dream Travel Plan**, to travel more and do it within your at-home cost of living. Everything you need is right here; just keep reading and, soon, you will be the travel expert giving advice.

Approach

Unlike most travel literature that tells you where to go and what to do, the Dream Travel Plan is a flexible, step-by-step system that shows you how to build and live out your custom-tailored travel plan at the lowest possible price. It works wherever you go and however you travel. The simplicity is in its layout, and it is so incredibly comprehensive and practical that you can use it for the rest of your life. With the Dream Travel Plan, you can travel today at the lowest possible price. As you continue to master all of the techniques described in the plan, you will eventually be able to visit places at a fraction of the going rate.

How the Dream Travel Plan works:

First: Make a list of the top 10 places you want to visit.

Next: Prioritize places on your list that are least expensive to visit today.

Finally: This book will show you how to one day visit places that are expensive to visit today at a fraction of the cost.

Your journey through this book will expose you to epic conquests pulled off by fellow travelers just like you. You will also find resources that will help you better prepare for your travels and warnings that will keep you out of trouble. In the back of this book, you will also find:

Appendix A: A fully-loaded list of travel resources called, "The Suitcase." It has hundreds of neatly organized options for flights, housing, transportation, and more! You will also find the most highly recommended travel websites, sorted from least to most expensive options so you can quickly find the best and least expensive options for you.

Appendix B: A Travel Planning Form that can fast-track your travel planning and get you traveling now, at a fraction of the going rate.

Appendix C: A travel writer's sales template to help you fund your trips by selling freelance articles about your adventures.

What Money Tells You about People

It's amazing what can you learn about people by watching how they handle their money. Back in college, I was a regular at wing night. I'd order 50 wings with a glass of milk and always had a blast. While my friends chuckled at me drinking milk in a bar, I was amused by what their spending habits told me about them.

One night, my friend Steve was passing through town and came out to join us. He worked hard, traveled a lot, did it in style, and paid big bucks to do it. Steve justified his spending by saying he deserved it. That night, Steve bought shots by the round, drank more than the others, and topped off his night with a chocolate eruption lava cake.

Dan was a wing night regular who was always on the go, ate healthy, and kept fit. He came out more for the conversation than the food. He'd have a beer or two and would pick at leftover wings. That night, Dan accepted Steve's shots, more out of politeness than desire.

On this night, Dan brought Tracy along. She was on a year-long sabbatical and had been traveling the world for 10 straight months. Tracy was the life of the table with amazing stories of visits to places like Rome, London, New York, and Las Vegas.

I found it interesting that Tracy nursed her beer for two hours, turned down Steve's shots, and munched on a veggie plate. When the bills came, Steve's was five times more than anyone else's. Tracy, on the other hand, was traveling more than any of us but had the lowest tab, and Dan's wasn't much higher than hers.

Who do you think had the most fun? It sure wasn't Steve. He spent the most but appeared dissatisfied as we left for the evening and seemed a bit peeved that the gang wasn't more excited about the generous shots he bought.

Moral of the Story

We all could have bought more, but we each had our reasons not to. This is the mindset you need to have, as a long-term traveler. Be smart with your money, and be relentless in your pursuit to hang onto it. Don't lose sight of what you need your money for so that you don't waste it on things you don't need. Know what's important to you, be it the view, the experience, the conversation, whatever …

All You Need is a mindset change. By that, I mean you need to disassociate how much you spend from the satisfaction derived. You then need to apply all your knowledge, resourcefulness, and creativity to spend lean (not cheap) so that when temptation appears with a price tag, you know your priorities, can distinguish needs from "nice-to-haves," and can make the most of what you have so you can afford more of what you need.

There are millions of wonders to see in the world and a million more ways to experience them. Trust me, there is no single place on earth that you have to see so badly that justifies spending $400-$500 a day. Instead, move those big-ticket trips down in priority, in favor of destinations you can visit inexpensively today. By giving the principles in this book time to work their magic, you can one day be able to visit those big-ticket destinations for the price of a staycation.

When you understand your priorities and keep your impulses in check, you can afford to loosen the purse strings every so often without worry. Aficionados pinch their budgets where it doesn't hurt so they can indulge more in their passions.

In the end, the travel bug carrying the least financial weight is the one that can fly furthest and longest. So be frugal, but don't lower yourself to save a dollar at any cost.

A Letter Written in the Moment

Dear Travel Bug (a.k.a. you),

First, please forgive my inability to adequately describe the euphoria I feel. Although words cannot do justice to the magical moment I'm experiencing, I will not allow it to deprive you of the thrill you so deserve to feel or the transformation that can change your life. I have found a secret passage through the financial barriers that hold so many travelers back, and the map is within these pages.

It's hard to believe that, a few years ago, I thought travel was inherently expensive and that I'd have to settle for one big trip a year. But that's history ... As I stroll the alleyways in Venice, a seismic shift happens inside me. As the sun sets behind St. Mark's Square, everything is perfect, and my daily concerns melt away, as I say to myself, "This is what life is about!" It's not the first time I have felt this way. It happened while I stood under the Christmas tree in Rockefeller Center. It happened again on the sandy white beaches of Boracay. And I know this feeling will occur on my next great adventure.

It's my deepest hope that you channel the inspiration within you and use the tools in this book to change your life. Once you arrive, you'll know exactly what I so passionately want to describe to you now.

As you learn to replicate this feeling at different times and in different places, you will have harnessed your passions. That is when you'll know the travel bug has finally bitten.

Your Fellow Travel Bug,

RUSSELL HANNON

Venice

PART I

Yours for the Taking

"Don't dream your life, live your dreams …"

– Miasha

1

Yes, You Can: Live Your Dreams

"The trouble is, you think you have time."

–Jack Kornfield, *Buddha's Little Instruction Book*

Know this ...

At this very moment, there are more amazing places to see and wonderful things happening in the world than you can possibly imagine. All you need to do is get there.

Neither the most eloquent words nor the latest technology can replicate the firsthand thrill of the moment. Eventually, you need to get out there and experience it yourself—kiss under the Eiffel Tower, feel the mist of the falls, hear the thundering roar of the waves, breathe the fresh mountain air, and see the sparkling big city sky lights from high above. The greatest moments in your life are apt to happen when you step off the treadmill of life. They are the once-in-a-lifetime experiences and the times you first lay your eyes on those majestic views.

"Congratulations, you just turned 100!" Now the bad news ... You've outlived all your friends and most of your family. You're so frail you can't dress yourself, let alone go to the washroom by yourself. You will now be spending the rest of your days in a nursing home, and you can only dream about all the places you longed to see but never got to. If only ...

The point is there are no second chances at life. Either we take steps to give ourselves a fighting chance to live our dreams, or we are likely to miss out on many of the wonders that were ours for the taking. The question is, "Are you doing what you need to do today so that you don't have regrets tomorrow?"

Conquer Your Fears

Perched atop the Peak of Panorama Mountain, my legs instantly turned into Jell-O.

"How will I ever get out of this one?" I asked myself, as I stared down the barrel of a double black diamond run. I was suddenly jolted with the realization that I was not the expert skier I thought I was. The problem was, I had already passed the point of no return, and there was no climbing back up the hill. To settle my quivering nerves, I closed my eyes, took a deep breath, and slowly opened them to the breathtaking view of a thousand mountain peaks. That's when inspiration found me in the unlikeliest form. From out of nowhere, a group of ski students suddenly whisked by me, following their instructor. They were wearing yellow bibs which reminded me of little ducklings following the mother duck and, one at a time, the little ducklings hopped over a ledge and fell out of sight.

I imagined how battered my pride would be, if I had to be rescued from the mountain as little ducklings whizzed by. That's when a seismic shift happened. I blocked out the dizzying heights and hardwired myself to focus only on where I wanted to be two seconds from now and what I had to do to get there. I made one turn and then another, focusing strictly on what I was doing at that moment. I kept my anxiety in check, and my confidence grew with each passing turn. Before I knew it, I had made it to the bottom—fully intact!

Had I not faced my fears on Panorama Mountain, I would be less likely to face those very same fears which can re-emerge at different times and in different places. Now, anytime I feel that fear creep in, I think back to that calming view of 1000 mountain peaks and how I harnessed it to blaze my own path.

Making It Happen

Achieving the unachievable requires you to scale barriers others aren't willing to climb. Even though this book is your blueprint to overcoming the financial barriers to travel, whether and how you use it will dictate whether or not you make it. Since you're reading this, I'm assuming that you're passionate about travel. If not, I don't expect to see you at the ultra-economical travel party because you won't have the drive to get there.

Those who are happiest focus more on their passions than their problems. Their attitude is what makes the difference between giving up and having a great time, regardless. Attitude is everything—it's a glass half full view of the world, and it comes from having a positive state of mind. If your first response is often negative, or you find yourself putting off things you want to do, consider that to be a telltale sign that your attitude is slipping.

Our Common Bond

I learned a lot about myself from someone I never met. He taught me a lot about you, too …

His name is Michael Losier, and his book, *The Law of Attraction*, explains that many of our perceptions are biases resulting from our personal experiences and limited knowledge of situations and circumstances. These misperceptions lead us astray, through the decisions we make and actions we take.

"I don't want to be here" was the unsettling feeling that suddenly crept into me, during my first visit to an underdeveloped country. As I looked out the window of my plane, descending on Manila, all I could see from the ocean to the horizon were dense slums. I was overcome with the feeling that it was unsafe and unsanitary, and my reflex was to stay close to my hotel. Eventually, I decided to explore the city and came to realize that I overreacted.

Next time that unsettling feeling overtakes you while traveling, challenge yourself to see whether it's really the place or circumstance that's causing it or whether it's actually your attitude that's making you feel that way.

Ignite Your Attitude

You can't bring the Bahamas back with you, but your attitude follows you everywhere. The difference between having a radiant glow and walking the streets like a zombie rests with the attitude you carry out the door each day. Whether you notice it or not, your attitude may be pulling you down. Anytime you feel yourself digressing, it's important to acknowledge it and look for the good in the bad.

Look at the bright side:

- The view is just as good on Tuesday as it is on Friday ... and less expensive, too!
- Ski resorts are not only cheaper on weekdays, you also have the hill to yourself.
- Locals are more receptive to tourists when their town is not being overtaken during peak season.

Mind over Matter

It doesn't matter how much you have, you'll never be satisfied unless you can disassociate how much you spend from the value of your experience. When you truly understand what makes you happy, it becomes easy to pinch your budget where it doesn't hurt so you don't need to pinch it where it does.

2

The Travel Bug, a Curious Creature

"Once the travel bug bites, there is no known antidote, and I know that I shall be happily infected for the rest of my life."

– Michael Palin

Once bitten, the travel bug forever changes you, making you highly contagious to spread it to others. All over the world, travel bugs are spreading their fever. This bug does not discriminate by age, race, life stage, or lifestyle. Some are wealthy and pampered, while others are underprivileged or poor.

Travel bugs understand there is no correlation between how much they spend and the pleasure derived. They pursue experiences over possessions and want to see the world firsthand to feel the exhilaration, channel the inspiration, and thrive from the rejuvenation that comes through travel. They appreciate diversity in all its forms and seek a deeper understanding of why people and things are as they are.

Signs the travel bug has bitten:

- You start planning your next trip as soon as you return from your last one.
- You live like a local, while abroad, and immerse yourself in the places you visit.
- You find inspiration through travel.
- You seek passionate experiences over things.
- Your greatest joys from travel come from the people you meet along the way.
- You pursue what you want and not what the world says you should be.
- You tend to wander off the beaten path, out of pure interest and curiosity.
- You are curious, generous, tolerant, open-minded, and accepting.
- You appreciate diversity, history, art, nature, and photography.
- You enjoy sharing your travel stories as much as you enjoy listening to others.
- Your most wonderful moments occur while doing the simplest things.
- You push beyond your comfort zone to confront your fears and doubts.
- You leave a little bit of yourself in each place you visit and take a little part of it with you.

Signs the travel bug has yet to bite:

- "Culture shock" describes your vacation.
- You leave without having met any locals or gotten any sense of how the locals live.
- Your trips tend to be tours of nine countries in 14 days.
- You drink too much, eat too much, spend too much, sleep too little, and return feeling exhausted and broke.

"Tourists don't know where they've been, travelers don't know where they're going."

– Paul Theroux

Tourist	vs.	Travel Bug
What you saw		How it made you feel
Floral shirt, fanny pack, shorts and high socks		No tacky shirts, high socks are for suits
You view the world from your perspective		You seek to learn about different cultures and understand different perspectives
You throw the budget out the window. "After all, I deserve it"		You live like a local and spend as you would at home
Naive, unfamiliar with local culture		You immerse yourself in local life

"If we could sell our experiences for what they cost us, we'd all be millionaires."

– Abigail Van Buren

The F.A.T. Travel Bug

After spending months holed up in a cubicle, watching friends post updates from the tropics, and flicking between Anthony Bourdain's shows and the Amazing Race, who can blame you for throwing the budget out the window, on the rare occasion you get to break loose and leave town. I call it budget amnesia; you are so travel-deprived that you go all out, as if the credit card bill will never come in. It's like a kid who eats all the Halloween candy in one sitting then feels awful afterward. In travel terms, overspending is overeating. To keep yourself from overeating, you need to stop depriving yourself from traveling for months (or years) at a time.

There are three main things that inflate your travel budget (or, as I say, make it F.A.T.) and keep you from traveling as much as you want to:

Food

If you can eat the way you do at home, while traveling, eating won't add to your costs of travel.

Accommodations

For long-term travel, the biggest factor that will make or break your budget is the cost of your accommodations. If you spend three weeks a year in hotels, you will dish out at least $3,000 more on those hotels than you would spend by staying in alternative accommodations that millions of travelers use every day.

Transportation

The cost of long-haul flights is often the show stopper that keeps people from booking a trip. Lucky for you, this book will show you how to land free flights, beat the best online fare, get around checked bag fees, and score ultra-inexpensive ground transportation.

First Person to Travel the World

Long lines at airports and cramped seats wouldn't bother the first person to travel around the world. More than 400 years ago, facing starvation, drowning, extreme weather, disease, and attack, the first person to travel around the world did so half by accident—and didn't pay a cent to do it either.

While some historians dispute who the first person to circle the globe was, here are the basic facts:

Ferdinand Magellan (we'll call him Fema) was a Portuguese explorer who ran shipping expeditions to the Spice Islands (modern day Indonesia). While there, he captured a slave to act as his translator, naming him "Enrique of Malacca."

Due to an increase in sea battles on trade routes, the King of Spain tasked Fema with finding an alternate sailing route to the Spice Islands. In 1519, Fema and Enrique set sail to the west to find an alternate shipping route.

Fast forward a year and a half, Fema and his expedition landed in the Philippines, and they were surprised at how well Enrique could speak with the Filipinos, suggesting he might have been born there.

During their stay, tensions rose between the expedition and the local natives, who butchered Fema in a beachside battle. With his master slain, Enrique considered himself free and took offense when the remaining expedition claimed that he now belonged to them. For that reason, Enrique conspired and turned an allied tribe against the remaining explorers. The night before their departure, the tribe invited the explorers to a feast and laid a violent ambush. (Always be leery when offered unlimited alcohol.)

A few lucky explorers escaped with their lives and continued on to the Spice Islands and, eventually, Portugal. Enrique stayed in the Philippines and was never heard from again.[1] So the debate is:

- If Enrique was born in the Philippines, he is the first person to travel around the world.
- If Enrique was born west of the Philippines, the title goes to those lucky few escapees. Not that they cared, they were lucky to be alive.

Overcome Your Transportation Barriers

If you've found yourself spending countless hours running mind-numbing searches on every website you can find, this book will restore your sanity with:

- The Fast Tracker, which shows you how to land the best price, depending on the scenario.
- A step-by-step guide on how to "Out-Negotiate the Priceline Negotiator."
- Ways to automate your search to get the best deals delivered to your inbox.

The Leech

Why is it so easy to be bad and overspend? Like any good story, there has to be a bad guy, and our bad guy is the leech that drains F.A.T. travel budgets, in the form of:

Hotel rack rates	Foreign visas	Currency conversion fees
Taxis	Airport taxes	Foreign transaction charges
Mobile roaming fees	Scams	Double occupancy billing
Restaurants	Parking	Inflated excursion prices
	Forced gratuities	

Symptoms

Ten years ago, I was covered with leeches and didn't even know it. I thought:

- The post-vacation credit card bill was normal
- Saving up for months was the price I had to pay to travel
- I had to settle for one big trip a year

The first time I noticed the leeches was in 2003, after a trip to Vegas. Despite flying on points and having a free place to stay, I somehow managed to blow five grand in eight days.

Diagnosis

This was a serious case of budget amnesia, where the leeches bled my travel budget dry, and I couldn't figure out where it had all gone.

The Cure

We often have to experiment before finding a cure. The first time I took a stand against high travel prices, I took the cheap path instead of the frugal one, opening a whole new can of worms in the process. No, I didn't run with the bulls without medical insurance, but I did lose $350 after purchasing a flight with a no change, no refund, no cancellation policy and later having to postpone my trip.

Cheap	vs.	Ultra-Economical
Piling five people to a room		Staying with friends and in apartment style accomodations
Living off "street meat" and fast food to keep costs down		Eating as well as when at home
Using a company phone strictly for personal use during summer vacation abroad		Using secure Wi-Fi connections for free, calling on Skype, FaceTime, and BBM
Using a hand-me-down suitcase held together with tie twists		Comparison shopping online to find a quality suitcase at an economical price

In the long run, cheap people pay three times over:

> **First** to get it,
>
> **Then again** because it only lasts half as long,
>
> **And finally** for the hassle of putting up with something they didn't want in the first place.

Those wrong turns taught me how to distinguish wants from needs. So I stopped staying in cheap motels in favor of fully furnished condos. I stopped traveling during high season and no longer bought things in overpriced, touristy areas. Eventually, I pulled off:

- A dozen free trips.
- Four separate trips to four of the world's most expensive cities, totalling a month, for under $2,000 (London, Monaco, New York, San Francisco).
- A four-month Vegas vacation on less than $500/ month.

Life costs money, and we will always have some F.A.T. in our travel budget. The goal is to not spend more than what the locals pay to live there. That translates to spending five times less than the average traveler.

3
The Machine That Changed the World

"He that idly loses 5 shillings worth of time, loses 5 shillings, and might as prudently throw 5 shillings into the river."

– Benjamin Franklin

Would you believe the best-selling book The Machine That Changed the World isn't about a machine at all? It's about a system. Would you believe this system can also get you traveling at a fraction of the going rate? Henry Ford was an early pioneer in the auto industry who hinted at the potential of this system in a striking statement in his 1922 book, My Life and Work, on founding the Ford Motor Company. In it, he said:

> *"The average farmer puts to a really useful purpose only about 5% of the energy he expends. ... Not only is everything done by hand, but seldom is a thought given to a logical arrangement.*
>
> *A farmer doing his chores will walk up and down a rickety ladder a dozen times. He will carry water for years instead of putting in a few lengths of pipe. His whole idea, when there is extra work*

to do, is to hire extra men. He thinks of putting money into improvements are [sic] an expense in time & money. ... It is wasted motion— wasted effort— that makes farm prices high and profits low."[2]

What's fascinating about Henry's example is how it carries over to travel. We waste hours searching for a better deal and pay too much in the end, anyway. But what's absolutely astounding is that the very things that revolutionized farming and manufacturing can also get you globetrotting at a fraction of the going rate, in a fraction of the time it would otherwise take.

Method to the Madness

To make the leap to ultra-economical travel, the following four lean management principles will empower you to consistently get you what you want at the right time, for the best price:

Eliminate unnecessary and time consuming activities, such as aimlessly scouring websites and spending hours comparing search results.

Simplify things so anyone can find the best results fast, including how to:

- Get the best price in 15 minutes flat for a range of travel scenarios and
- Out-negotiate the Priceline negotiator.

Reduce how much money you need to spend to take that dream vacation.

Integrate everything for exponential results. This is getting a free flight and free accommodations while also bypassing checked bag fees, ATM charges, and roaming fees—all on the same trip.

These four principles are the foundations of lean management. It's my area of expertise, and it's going to change your travel destiny. The concept of lean is to eliminate wasteful tasks that fail to save you time and money, without taking away from your end goal. It's what catapulted Toyota from a small car company to the world's largest automaker. The secret to Toyota's success was to cut three types of wasteful tasks from its processes, known in Japanese as:

1. **Muri** (a.k.a. ineffective): The first decision most travelers make when planning a trip is often the wrong one—it's deciding to go to the same places as everyone else, at the same time. The "Dream Travel Plan" and "Seven Passports" show you how to effectively plan your travels, while saving time and money.

2. **Mura** (a.k.a. consistently inconsistent and ineffective): The Fast Tracker lays out step-by-step how to quickly find the best price by travel scenario so you can quickly and consistently get the best price.

3. **Muda** (a.k.a. wasting energy): For more than a decade, I continuously enhanced and honed the systems in this book by continuously replacing the old way of doing things, anytime I found a better way to travel more and better on less.

4

Your Seven Passports to the World

Any travel deal that you, I, or anyone has ever had was the result of one of just seven things. Before you look at them, think back to any travel deal you ever got, then pinpoint which of the following travel passports played a hand in your travel deal.

People Means Knowledge Creativity Flexibility Adaptability Pure Luck

Travel Passport #1: People

Take everyone you know, add everyone they can put you into contact with, and what you have is your network. Your network is your million dollar travel rolodex, and many travel bugs have seen the world using this one passport alone. Having a free place to stay is just the beginning ... The greatest times in my life were the result of the people I was with, and the real magic of the people passport is the satisfaction you get from connecting with others.

Garden Your Network

Things come easier to those who constantly garden their network, whether it's finding a job, meeting your spouse to be, or making connections that can save you money on your next trip. Amazing things happen when you position yourself to meet people, offer simple acts of kindness, and reciprocate to those who help you. It can be as simple as offering a helping hand, washing the dishes in thanks for dinner, or offering a symbolic gift (it could even include sharing tips from this book). These things are inexpensive, easy to do, and make everyone feel good.

You will know you're on the right path when you catch yourself saying, "I can't believe how many amazing people I meet in random ways" and "I'm blessed to have so many wonderful people in my life." When you live like this and the time comes that you need something, you will be overwhelmed at how many people will step up to offer a helping hand.

Even if you aren't traveling, you can garden your travel network by attending local travel meet-ups and by hosting travelers through travel hospitality networks (more on these later).

Leveraging Your People Passport

Anytime you travel as part of a group, take the time to ask everyone what they can contribute. You will often learn that someone in your group may be:

- A flight attendant with extra buddy passes for free flights.
- A hotel employee who qualifies for discounted rates.
- A business traveler with elite status or who is entitled to corporate rates.

How to Waste a Day in Monaco

I insist that you politely impose. There was a time when I didn't want to impose ... so, instead of taking up my caretaker's offer to help if I needed anything, I wasted my last day in Monaco trying to download a map of Italy onto my portable GPS. I didn't have an internet connection in my flat so I made my way to the only cyber café in town. It was just my luck that the internet connection tripped each time my download neared 50% complete, forcing me to start over.

Seven hours later, I had no map, no smile and, when I returned to my flat, the universe worked its magic in the form of a ringing phone. It was my flat's caretaker, and she wanted to know how I was making out. When I mentioned my problem, she had her son Pierre-Louis invite me over, and we had a wonderful conversation, as I downloaded my map.

Had I leveraged my network and called my caretaker about my problem, I would have had one extra day to enjoy Monaco.

Travel Passport #2: Means

Non-financial means get you things you would otherwise have to pay for. I like to say that ultra-economical travel requires you to have "a bucket of frugalness and a barrel of resourcefulness," which can get you a lot further than simple frugality. Resourcefulness comes in the form of charisma, persuasion, an ability to negotiate and leverage your purchasing power, memberships, preferential status, and finding ways to get around the system.

Amy is a web developer who took a career break to travel around the world for a year. When the owner of a hostel in Malaysia learned of her web development skills, he offered her a free stay and a flight to her next destination. During her trip, Amy also worked on a company's website for 12 days and received in return: free accommodations, including breakfast and lunch each day, a four-day cruise, a hot air balloon ride at cost, and 250 Euros cash.

Travel Rewards

If you would like to pull off a few free trips each year, you need to join the travel rewards party. Designed to drive buyer loyalty and allow vendors to track buying patterns, many loyalty programs offer big-time incentives upon signing up, in the form of points you can redeem for free flights and hotel nights. Just about every company has a loyalty program these days, with the advantage going to those that offer the most lucrative incentives.

Earn Points by Living Life

It's easy to earn rewards points for nearly everything you purchase. All you need to do this is:

- Sign up for a credit card that awards you points for every dollar spent.
- Charge as many of your day-to-day purchases to your credit card as you can (and, of course, pay your credit card balance in full every month).
- Prioritize vendors that have loyalty programs over others that don't.

Stockpiling Rewards Points – The Basics

Anytime you buy anything, make sure you're enrolled in that company's loyalty program. It's always free to sign up, and it only takes a few minutes. The trick is to enroll before making your purchase so that you earn points for that first purchase. Even if you never purchase anything from that vendor again, you may be able to transfer those points to a partner loyalty program (more on this later).

I have built mountains of points by buying everything (and I mean everything) on credit cards that earn me points per dollar spent.

Dining Rewards

The American Airlines Advantage Dining Program (aa.com) offers five points per dollar spent at affiliated restaurants.

Shopping Rewards

Rewards programs partner with retailers as much as they do with travel suppliers. With the emergence of online retail, online stores are luring shoppers from brick and mortar stores with enticing reward incentives amounting to five, ten, and even fifteen points per dollar spent. To keep on top of where you can get the most points for your purchases, evreward.com is a website that shows you reward program promotions offered by store. You also earn extra points by purchasing directly through loyalty program online malls.

Sign-up Bonuses

Credit card companies and banks will go all out to get their cards into your hands, by offering you sign-up bonuses in the form of free round trip flights, hotel nights, free and inexpensive flight companion passes, instant elite status, VIP airport lounge access, free checked-bags, travel and collision insurance, and the list goes on. Even better, many credit cards waive your annual fee the first year, to further entice you to sign up. Some cards even release their sign-up bonus to you multiple times, if you re-enroll after canceling.

Some banks offer sign-up bonuses for opening a bank account. I once took advantage of a promotion at a bank offering a free flight for opening a checking account. I later decided to close the account and, when I saw the promotion run again the following year, I opened another account and qualified for the sign-up bonus a second time!

For a list of the best credit card sign-up bonuses, visit the "FUND YOUR TRAVELS" section of breakthetravelbarrier.com.

Stockpile Points without Buying Anything

Twice a year, I get giddier than a kid on Christmas day. I sit back with my tablet and a glass of wine, while I browse credit card sign-up promotions that offer both:

i. No annual fee for the first year, and

ii. A sign-up bonus that I can redeem for at least:

- One free round trip flight, or
- Two hotel nights

It's important that you shop around, as some cards offer significantly larger sign-up bonuses than others. Knowing it would be a lean management sin to waste time looking up individual credit cards one at a time, you will find a list of the best credit card sign-up bonuses that also waive the first year annual fee at breakthetravelbarrier.com under "FUND YOUR TRAVELS." Before making this list, I used to turn to these websites for information on credit card sign-up bonuses:

nerdwallet.com: Travel credit cards

thepointsguy.com: Rewards cards

rewardscanada.ca: Top travel rewards credit cards (Canada)

Every year, this ritual lands me a handful of free flights and hotel nights. To see how I pulled off one of them, scan this QR code:

Although the exact promotions I used in this video might have expired or may not be available in your area, you can see how ridiculously easy it is to score free trips through credit card sign-up bonuses. If only Santa was this generous ...

Minimum Spend

Sign-up bonuses come with a few strings attached. These conditions are generally reasonable and are well worth the effort for what you get in return.

Credit cards require you to charge a minimum dollar amount to your credit card, within a set timeframe, before releasing a sign-up bonus to you. Although minimum spend requirements vary by card, they average out to $3,000 in spend over the first three months, or $5,000 for business cards. To meet minimum spending requirements without much problem:

1. Don't sign up to more than one or two cards at a time so that you don't stretch your ability to meet the minimum spend requirements.

2. Charge everything you can to your credit card, on the condition that you can afford to pay it in full every month. Consider renewing your insurance and gym fees in one annual lump sum payment, and offer to pay any recreational league dues then collect the fees from your teammates.

3. If you travel for business, charge your travel expenses to your personal credit card and later claim your expenses.

Sign-up bonuses offered for opening a bank account generally require you to meet the following conditions:

1. Set up your paycheck for direct deposit into your new account.

2. Pay at least one bill directly from your new account.

3. Keep the account open for at least three months.

I always hear from people who say it isn't worth jumping through all these hoops. The way I see it, $33 in monthly fees plus two hours of my time is a small price to pay for a free, round trip flight anywhere in the continental U.S. or Canada.

"What if my day-to-day expenses aren't enough to cover minimum spend?"

Don't worry, you needn't go on a shopping spree or buy things you don't need. You can apply cash payments toward your minimum spend. Let's say you owe someone $50 for softball fees or the March Madness basketball pool. To apply that cash payment to your credit card, PayPal and Amazon Payments allow you to transfer funds from your credit card to send payments to other account holders.

1. Simply open an account with PayPal or Amazon Payments and set up your credit card information on file.

2. When you owe someone money, instead of paying cash, simply transfer the funds from the credit card on your account to that person. Currently, these services have caps on the amounts you can transfer via personal payments. To prevent abusive churning, Amazon monitors private payments to see

that they stay within $1,000 a month (for more on churning, see page 53). For this reason, it's important to familiarize yourself with PayPal's and Amazon's user agreements, which specify their terms and conditions of use.

FAQ: "Will I ruin my credit, if I sign up to multiple credit cards?"

I can tell you from personal experience that signing up for a handful of credit cards nudged my credit score down a few points, but my score still ranked as excellent and it rebounded to its prior level within a year.

WARNING

Credit card leveraging only works if you pay your credit card in full every month. If not, interest charges will wipe out the value of any rewards you earn and can erode your credit score at the same time. I pay my credit cards in full and on time every month and so should you.

Getting Around Annual Renewal Fees

As your credit card's annual renewal date approaches, call customer service and tell them you might want to cancel. Customer service agents almost always offer incentives in a last ditch effort to keep you from canceling, by either waiving your annual fee or by offering free points.

TIP: Anytime you find yourself a few hundred points shy for a reward redemption, you can often top up your points for free. Just call customer service, say you are a few points shy of a rewards redemption, and ask what options there are to round up your points balance. The agent will give you the option of buying points, to which you should politely respond, "Thank you, but that's too expensive. Are there any other options? I just need a few hundred points."

Agents can often release small amounts of points, without getting higher authorization, so you want to keep the agent on the phone and be nice, in hopes of being rewarded with a top-up.

Credit Card Travel Benefits

Sign-up bonuses aside, credit cards offer a plethora of travel benefits. Here are four websites devoted to travel rewards programs so you can quickly compare cards and find those that offer the best benefits for you:

- boardingarea.com: Offers creative ways to earn travel rewards.
- cardsfortravel.com: Compares cards by reward type and rates the best overall (Canada and U.S.).
- rewardscanada.ca: Is devoted to Canadian frequent flyer and travel rewards programs.
- thepointsguy.com: Specializes in how to travel the world on points.

Make a Mountain, Not an Anthill Farm

In the world of travel rewards, one big pot is better than many small ones. When all else is equal, try to stockpile the bulk of your points into programs that:

- Are affiliated with the travel suppliers you most often use.
- Offer the most flexible terms of use.
- Allow you to transfer points at a 1-to-1 ratio.

Loopholes

Just as the good old days of paying your mortgage with your credit card have ended, anytime a great loophole emerges, it's just a matter of time before it gets shut down. To get in on the next loophole, follow travel experts on social media and sign up to their newsletters to receive breaking updates. I recommend:

flyertalk.com: For the latest frequent flier program changes.

milepoint.com: Where travelers share information about reward programs on an online chat forum.

thepointsguy.com: For amazing deal alerts.

Hotel Points Promotions

If you ever run into me in a hotel, chances are I'll either be checking in or checking out that very day. Hotel rewards are often awarded per separate stay, defined as a distinct check-in and check-out, regardless of how long you stay. Because of this, I've earned boatloads of points by staying in different hotels in close proximity on a daily basis. This may sound like a lot of work, but when you tally up all the points you can earn for the 30 minutes it takes each day, what you save in future hotel costs can be worth more than what you would earn working your day job during that time.

Transferring Points

Rewards programs increasingly encourage you to transfer points between programs, with promotions that offer bonus points for doing so. The problem is many programs devalue your points, when you transfer them.

Let's say you get a 40% bonus for transferring 10,000 points. The bonus will be calculated once your points have been transferred and only after they are subject to a 50% devaluation. The net result is a loss of 3,000 points despite getting a 40% bonus. The only time it makes sense to do this is when:

i. You can transfer your points at a net one-to-one ratio or better.

ii. You know you will never redeem points from a particular program.

Common Terms and Conditions

- A minimum number of points must be transferred (for example, 5,000 points).
- Transfers must be done in set increments (of 1,000 or 5,000 points, for instance).
- There are often limits to how many points you can transfer.

Some credit card reward programs allow you to transfer points to affiliated reward programs at a one-to-one ratio. A number of Chase and American Express rewards cards work this way, as does Canada's RBC Avion card. By using these cards, you can:

- Redeem your points with any affiliated travel supplier.
- Increase the shelf life of your points, as they are not subject to aging or expiry until after they are allocated to a loyalty program. Some loyalty programs stipulate that points automatically expire if they go unused for more than a set period of time. By refraining from allocating your points to a program until you plan to redeem them, you protect your points from the risk of expiring.

Keep on Top of It All

Things get complicated when you have dozens of rewards accounts. To keep on top of it all, set up a folder in the cloud with all your rewards program information so that you can access it anytime from anywhere. For each loyalty program, indicate the account or member number, password, and website address.

Churning

Churning is the act of moving digital currency (electronic funds, points, gift card balances, or debit card reloads) through multiple channels without actually buying anything. Imagine walking through a revolving door knowing that you will get five dollars for each full rotation you make until you stop. If you're like me, you'd probably spin until you're so dizzy you can no longer stand or until the door gets jammed.

In 2013, Americans churned rewards points by purchasing Vanilla reload debit cards at office supply stores using Chase Ink Bold and Ink Plus cards that offered five points per dollar charged at those stores. Purchasers then transferred the balance of their Vanilla reload card to an AMEX Bluebird account so they could withdraw the balance as cash and repay the credit card they used to purchase it in the first place. Then they did it all over again.

Loopholes like this never last long. In this case, the office supply stores closed the loophole by implementing a cash-only purchase policy for Vanilla reload cards.

Be First to Know

As reward programs and creative promotions continue to increase and evolve, so will the number of loopholes and opportunities. The key is to learn of them quickly enough to cash in on the bonanza. To stay in the know about the latest loopholes and emerging trends, I maintain a list of travel experts who specialize in finding loopholes. You can find the list at breakthetravelbarrier.com under "Resources > FUND YOUR TRAVELS." They include:

thepointsguy on Facebook and Twitter

rocketmiles.com

pointshound.com

Next time opportunity strikes, you will be in a position to load up on points.

Leveraging Alliances

Most airlines, hotels, and resorts are members of alliances that honor the points and priority status of alliance members meaning you can:

1. Redeem rewards in places not serviced by your provider.
2. Cherry-pick from the most generous alliance members to fast-track your way to elite status, accelerate your point growth, and fly further on fewer points.

For a complete list of alliances and alliance members, visit the following alliance websites:

- Airlines: One World (oneworld.com), Sky Team (skyteam.com), Star Alliance (staralliance.com)
- Hotels: Carlson (clubcarlson.com), Five-star (fivestaralliance.com), Hilton (hilton.com), Hyatt (hyatt.com), IHG (ihg.com), Starwood (spg.com)

Rules of Thumb

- Treat rewards points like cash.
- When buying something from a vendor for the first time, always sign up for their loyalty program.
- Pay for everything on credit cards that offer points per dollar spent, and pay your balance in full each month.
- Avoid companies that have no loyalty program, in favor of others that do.
- Capitalize on credit cards that offer big sign-up bonuses and waive the annual fee your first year. For a list of cards meeting this criteria, visit "FUND YOUR TRAVELS" at breakthetravelbarrier.com

Travel Passport #3: Knowledge

For every great deal you ever had, there were dozens of better ones you didn't know about. That is why knowledge is power. It gives you options, saves you money, keeps you out of trouble, enhances your experience, and gets you more for less.

What You Don't Know Can Cost You

Every day, anywhere you go, you are at risk of being overcharged. You need to know what your blind spots are and cover them, to protect yourself from unnecessary spending. If knowledge is power, then power comes from getting the information you need at the precise time you need it. Luckily for you, you just happen to be living in the midst of the most profound revolution since the invention of writing. It's the knowledge revolution, and it has opened the floodgates of instant access to anything you need to know, when you need to know it. Those who come out ahead in the knowledge revolution may not be the strongest or even the smartest, but they will be those who are fastest to adapt and adopt.

Once you find valuable information, you can instantly capture and neatly organize it in a few clicks and later retrieve it anytime from anywhere online.

Find Anything

To set up your custom-tailored travel search engine, seek travel experts who specialize in the types of deals you're looking for and sign up to their newsletter and twitter feeds:

cardsfortravel.com: Covers the latest credit card rewards promotions.

momondo.com: Sends lowest price fare alerts.

nomadicmatt.com: Offers budget travel advice and travel deals.

boardingarea.com: Shows you ways to accelerate your travel rewards earnings.

Shermanstravel.com: Publishes its weekly top 25 travel deals.

thepointsguy.com: Shows you how to travel first class on points.

travelzoo.com: Offers great deals on hotels, restaurants, golf, spas, and excursions.

rewardscanada.ca: Is devoted to Canadian rewards programs.

For a directory of travel newsletters, visit “BEST PRICE” at breakthetravelbarrier.com. If sifting through newsletters is not for you, you can also:

1. Go to ifttt.com (**If t**his **t**hen **t**hat.com) and set up a command to search for anything you want to find online. For example, you can set up commands that say:

    - “If Craigslist has a condo for rent in Scottsdale < $1,000/ month, copy and e-mail the link to me.”
    - “If my email receives a travel notification, load it to Evernote.”
    - “If a travel deal is posted meeting specific criteria, send it to: janedoe@gmail.com.”

2. Have all your newsletters sent to a virtual concierge who can filter through them for what you are looking for. A virtual concierge can do anything for you that can be done online or remotely. By leveraging remote technology that allows you to see currency and labor cost differences by country, you can hire a virtual concierge in a low-cost country at a fraction of what it would cost to hire someone locally. To master the art of outsourcing tasks to virtual assistants in low-cost countries, I highly recommend you read *“The 4-Hour Workweek,”* by Timothy Ferriss.

Where to Find a Virtual Concierge

asksunday.com

elance.com

fiverr.com

getfriday.com

peopleperhour.com

Remember Everything

How often do you learn of something amazing, only to later forget about it? By using any of the following solutions, you can capture, organize, and access data anytime, from any computer in the world:

Delicious.com: Save websites and tag them with bookmarks, notes, or free-form text.

Evernote.com: Capture and tag anything (text, audio, websites, documents, pictures).

Pinterest.com: "Pin" websites, articles, pictures, and videos and share them with your social network.

Anytime you come across information that you may need to call upon one day, use followupthen.com to send yourself an email reminder at the precise time you need that information. For example, let's say you are planning to catch a show on August 9th, and someone told you about a box office that sells same-day show tickets for half price.

Simply:

1. Capture the box office information in an email.
2. Send the email to '9august9am@followupthen.com'.
3. On August 9th, you will receive an email at 9 a.m. with the box office information.

I also use followupthen.com to reminder myself to search for promotions and apply for credit cards with hefty sign-up bonuses.

Cyber Monday

Cyber Monday is the Monday following U.S. Thanksgiving and is known as one of the most expensive travel days of the year. Ironically, it is also one of the best days of the year to find amazing travel deals online. Cyber Monday is the internet's version of Black Friday. Since most travel is booked online, visit your favorite travel websites on Cyber Monday, as they will likely advertise Cyber Monday deals on their homepage. Cybermondaydealslive.com and hugecybermondaydeals.com are websites that act as billboards that broadcast the best Cyber Monday deals. Simply go to their Travel section to look for deals that interest you. You will also want to keep an eye out for "Power Hour" super sales where websites offer killer deals on bookings made during a one-hour window.

Keep It Simple – Automate

The One Year Advance-Notice Deal

Last minute deals sometimes repeat themselves each year. Next time you come across a killer last-minute deal that you cannot take advantage of, use "CTA" to land that deal next time it comes around:

C – Capture the deal. Snap a picture, write a note, copy a link, or record your voice.

T – Tag the file to Evernote so that you can easily find it later. For example, I tagged a last-minute travel deal to Cuba under the key words: "Travel Deals – Last Minute – Cuba."

A – Automate: From Evernote, send your note to "10months@followupthen.com." Ten months later, an email will land in your inbox reminding you to look for that last-minute deal to pop up again.

Who would have imagined 25 years ago that, for the price of a phone plan, you could automate searches that sort, organize, and deliver exactly what you need, precisely when you need it?

Travel Passport #4: Flexibility

Being flexible can make the difference between landing a good deal and a great one.

"We'll take the cheapest flight out of town, please." Tara and her husband were an overworked couple and had not thought about traveling much, until a last-minute opportunity arose for them to take vacation at the same time. They decided to go to the airport and take the cheapest flight out of town, which turned out to be a $59 one-way flight to Minneapolis. Once there, they did the same thing again and hit pay dirt with an $89 flight to Miami, where they checked into a cozy hotel and asked the clerk if he knew of any deals in town. The clerk instructed them to go the port, where departing cruise ships sell off empty cabins at the last minute for rock-bottom prices. This landed them a week-long, all-inclusive Caribbean cruise with an ocean view cabin for $300 each.

But this is where the story changes. The moment they boarded that ship, they traded in their flexibility and were nickel-and-dimed with daily fees, surcharges, and extras for activities and excursions. When their cruise ended, they only had one day to get home in time for work so they had to pay a premium to get the exact flight they needed.

Cruise ship legislation has tightened since Tara's expedition, and all passengers must be registered and must also provide a photo ID at least 72 hours prior to departure. But I still love sharing her story, as it demonstrate how the flexibility passport can giveth and taketh away, once we trade in our flexibility.

Good things come to those who wait, and flexibility is an offensive stance, where you keep your options open so you can capitalize on unexpected opportunities that arise. Just as the fastest rabbit wins the race, the best deals go to those most able to pounce on them. Let's say you get an email about a flash sale for a round-trip flight to Frankfurt for $344. The 5% of us who are flexible enough to jump on that deal can get to Europe much more cheaply than the other 95% who aren't. Even if you have no interest in seeing Frankfurt, you can use this deal to get to Europe then continue on to wherever you want to go.

Travel Agents

Flexibility comes in many forms, and if you're a traveler whose schedule can change on a moment's notice, booking fees are well worth the price charged for 24/7 support, flexible change policies, and pre-negotiated terms and rates with certain travel suppliers.

If the rates you are getting through your travel agent are higher than those you get using this book, you need to either find another travel agent or invest the time to show the agent where and how to get the prices you expect. By sharing your secrets (and even this book), there's no reason your agent can't replicate your brilliance. Once a travel agent understands your needs and travel systems, the luxury of having 24/7 access to an agent with all your personal information on file not only saves you time and hassle, it can also be a godsend in an emergency.

The benefits of using a travel agent vary slightly by agency but generally include:

- 24/7 emergency assistance, whether you lose your wallet, passport, or miss your flight.
- An international toll-free number you can call from anywhere in the world.
- An agent who knows your preferences, offers personal attention, and saves you time.
- Purchase protection that reimburses you, should a travel supplier go bankrupt after you pay.
- Someone to check in with if you are traveling solo or visiting unstable parts of the world to say you're OK.
- Knowledge of certain destinations and insight that can help you.

What to Look For In a Travel Agency

- 24-hour service, including an off-hour emergency line.
- A toll-free international number.
- Prompt replies to your phone calls.

When you set up your account with a travel agent, provide all your loyalty program and credit card information, along with your passport, driver's license information, and preferences such as room type, seat location, and any nit-picky wants you may have. For example, my file shows that I prefer rooms with a mini fridge, that I want aisle seats for daytime flights and window seats on red eyes, I pay for Marriott bookings and international purchases with my Marriott Rewards card, I pay for IHG bookings with my IHG card, and I pay for Alaska Airlines bookings with my Alaska Airlines credit card. Everything else goes on my American Express card. That isn't so complicated is it?

Corporate Travel Agencies

If you work for a company that employs a corporate travel agency, you can get preferred corporate rates by booking your personal travel through them with your personal credit card. Two companies I worked for even encouraged employees to book their personal travel through their corporate travel agent. I think they should have listed this in the company benefits package as a perk!

Personal Concierge

When renting vehicles, opt for ones that come with in-car personal concierge services, such as On-Star, BMW Assist, and MBrace. This way, if you need help finding inexpensive accommodations, your concierge will do all the leg work to find you the best last-minute deal.

Travel Passport #5: Adaptability

A sister to flexibility, adaptability is a defensive stance, where you make the most of the hand you've been dealt. You will inevitably hit bumps, as you travel, and the fewer means you have to work with, the more adaptable you need to be.

Your willingness to adapt will dictate whether you can turn negatives into positives and will make the difference between having an amazing time, regardless of the circumstances, or a miserable trip to forget.

Travel Passport #6: Creativity

The creativity passport is my favorite of the bunch because of the sensational ways it has scored me countless discounts by helping me see beyond the obvious. Although you can certainly use my creative tricks, you will benefit even more by tapping into your creative genius to find opportunities in your unique situations. Creativity is more of an art than a science, therefore it isn't as easy to teach. The best coaches and insiders can only take you so far; you eventually need to take over at the controls. So, enjoy the creative examples that start on page 192, and let them inspire you to tap into the countless opportunities that are waiting to be discovered.

Travel Passport #7: Pure Luck

Pure luck is the trip you won. It's the black sheep of the travel passports because you can't plan on it or control it. For these reasons, this is the only time we will talk about pure luck. So, if you know someone who is waiting on the lottery to take their dream trip, flip the odds into their favor and get them this book.

"How Can These Travel Passports Help Me?"

Think back to the best travel deal you ever landed, and imagine getting that same deal or better on every trip you take for the rest of your life. Once you understand the conditions that give rise to an outcome, you can crack the code to ultra-economical travel by replicating those conditions for future trips.

You need to exercise your passports just like muscles. Depending on your circumstances, you may need to work more or less than others to get your passports firing on all cylinders. Some passports yield bigger and faster results than others. You can get immediate results with flexibility, but it will not save you as much over the long term as the people passport, which takes more time to build.

Although you only need one passport to land a great deal, by leveraging all the passports together at the same time, you can put your travel plan into hyper speed. No, you will not be able to spend the summer in five-star accommodations for the price of camping, but you can absolutely land a handful of free nights in five-star hotels each year. As you gain momentum, you will naturally offset many of your traditional travel costs, land better prices than others, and pull off an occasional free trip.

It won't be long before your family and friends notice that you appear to be traveling beyond your means when, in fact, you will simply be traveling, staying longer, and spending less.

Passports in Action

My Ultra-Economical European Escapade People

My people passport once landed me ten days in a furnished flat in Monaco, and all I had to pay was a $225 cleaning fee. During that trip, my people passport helped me further, when my caretaker had me over to her son's place so I could use his internet connection to download a map onto my GPS.

As I struggled to find my way from Monaco to the freeway, I stopped into a service station, greeted a person "en francais" with a bumper sticker that read, "I ♥ Montreal," and asked him for directions. Not only did he give me directions, he also:

- Personally led me to the freeway.
- Referred me to the best dollar-for-dollar value hotel in Venice.

- Explained Venice's ferry system, along with where to buy ferry passes and how to navigate the city.
- Gave me his number, instructing me to call him if I had questions or needed help along my way.
- Called me every few hours to see where I was and tell me what landmarks and turnoffs to look for.

If this isn't the most hospitable person in the world, I need to meet the person who is.

Knowledge

For any knowledge I lacked about the places I was visiting, I made up for it through the knowledge of others. Since my European friends had already been to Oktoberfest, I let them take care of the logistics. While I was in the south of France, I benefited from the knowledge and connections of my caretaker and my newfound friend with the Montreal bumper sticker.

What you don't know can hurt you. Had I known that taxis in many European countries start running the meter the moment they arrive (as opposed to when you embark), I would not have run up a 25 Euro fare before even embarking.

Means

To get to Europe, I flew to Nice on rewards points and bought a separate round trip flight from Nice to Munich on a regional budget airline.

I cut the cost of my car rental by booking it through my company's corporate travel agent to get a corporate rate with unlimited mileage.

By having an unlocked cell phone, I bought a SIM card from lefrenchmobile.com and got a plan with rates comparable to what locals pay.

While on route to Venice, instead of paying for a hotel in Milan, I redeemed IHG rewards points that I had built up through business travel to get a free room.

To keep my cost of eating on par with my at-home grocery budget, I bought groceries when I stayed in flats with kitchens. (When staying in hotels, I opt for ones that offer free continental breakfasts and pack a banana and a bagel to snack on throughout the day. I then stop into restaurants to have dinner, shortly before restaurant lunch specials wind up.)

To keep the cost of the Munich hotel room in check during Oktoberfest, we bunked four people into a room with two queen beds, a couch that was big enough to sleep on, and a futon.

To save money on our commute, we rode the train directly from the airport at a bulk rate by purchasing eight rail tickets (we needed four) and selling the extra tickets at the bulk rate to people waiting in line.

Flexibility

In one instance, had I not gone to Oktoberfest at the same time as my friends, it would have cost an arm and a leg more for accommodations. In another, by not having any fixed commitments, I took advantage of the last minute advice I received on the best value hotel in Venice.

Adaptability

A taxi fare got out of control in Milan when the driver ran the meter for 10 minutes in the parking lot, before I even embarked. So I decided to not get in and forgo drinking that night. Instead, I drove to the restaurant, which saved me a bundle.

Creativity

By taking advantage of the complimentary checked bag services in Monaco's casinos, I checked my backpack so that I could wander the streets and gardens without it.

Summary

By leveraging all of these passports, while on one trip, I visited three cities for less than what most people pay to visit one of them. Was any of this luck? Not a chance. It was ultra-economical travel.

Student Travel

Class, welcome to Student Travel 101.

You'll want to take careful notes during this crash course because, if you score an "A," you will be able to travel significantly more than your fellow classmates on the same budget.

The first thing you need is an internationally recognized student discount card that officially recognizes your student status worldwide. According to the International Student Identification Card (ISIC), over 4.5 million students use this card each year to get student discounts while traveling, for shopping, travel expenses, restaurants, attractions, and entertainment. Full-time students of any age qualify for this card. If you are not in school, the International Youth Travel Card (IYTC) is available to anyone under 26 and offers many of the same benefits. You will find a detailed list of benefits and instructions on how to get one of these cards at isic.org.

Government and travel operators alike have programs that make student and youth travel affordable, including programs that make it easy for people under 30 to get international work visas.

College-Funded Travel

Many colleges set funds aside for students to attend conferences as delegates. Many students have no idea these programs exist so, if you can sell the school on the value of sending you to an educational conference, odds are good your trip may get funded through your school.

One program I recommend is Best Delegate (bestdelegate.com) which is a program that gives students the opportunity to participate in mock United Nations (UN) sessions, learn how the UN works, and develop skills for diplomatic discussion and negotiation. Sessions take place all over the U.S., including in the actual UN assembly hall in New York.

If you want to attend an educational conference or workshop but cannot get funded by your school, you can set up an online crowdfunding profile on a crowdfunding website, such as fundmytravel.com, and share it through your social network asking for contributions to further your education. For details on how to set up an effective crowdfunding profile, go to page 167.

Student Travel Websites

itravelosophy.com is an international travel operator for students and teachers planning long-term trips to Asia, Africa, the Middle East, and Europe.

letsgo.com is loaded with blogs, videos, and travel books by student travelers.

rotary.org is a volunteer organization for student exchanges.

statravel.com is a full service travel provider that helps students plan every step of their trip, from getting an international student card, travel insurance, international phone, and credit cards to booking their trip.

studentuniverse.com keeps costs low by buying group travel packages in bulk and and offering travel planning services to youth aged 18 to 25.

PART II

Build Your Dream Travel Plan

"A journey of a thousand miles
begins with a single step."

– Lao Tzu

START HERE, for a more effective, less expensive, 21st century way of traveling. No matter how many travel books, systems, articles, blogs, or advice you've come by, the Dream Travel Plan will not only amaze you—it will change your travel destiny.

5
Know Yourself

It is said:

> "If you know yourself and your enemies, you shall not be imperiled in even a hundred battles. If you know yourself but not your enemies, you will win one and lose one. If you do not know either, you shall always be imperiled."
>
> – *The Art of War*

Measure and Monitor Your Spend

To truly know how much money this book will save you, you first need to know how much you've spent traveling to date. Just like dieting and exercise, you need to:

I. **Weigh yourself:** Every trip, measure how much you've spent.

II. **Assess** what you had to spend and where you could have cut back.

III. **Set your budget,** which isn't what you can afford but what you need to spend. That number is a lot less than you think it has to be.

IV. **Diet:** Shed the F.A.T. from your travel budget with a diet of the Dream Travel Plan.

V. **Get back on the scale:** Track where you've cut back, by how much, and why. If you aren't happy with the result, give the travel passports and Dream Travel Plan time to work their magic and keep moving forward.

Define Your Travel Type

Saving a few dollars is all for whatnot, if you don't get what you want from your travels. This is why it's important to define your travel type before you build your Dream Travel Plan. It's the foundation everything else is built on so you can save money without compromising what's important to you. To define your travel type, pick the dominant trait that best describes you in each of the following questions. At the end of the survey, you will find instructions that show you how to tally your result. You can ignore the numbers to the right of each option, for now.

1. I travel to:

a) Relax, unwind, and recharge. (6, 7)

b) Live it up at night. (1, 2, 3, 4)

c) Keep on the go all day and see as much as I can. (1, 2, 5, 6, 7)

d) Burn the candle on both ends. I'll sleep when I get home. (1, 2, 3)

2. I tend to drink:

a) Champagne or premium drinks. (1, 2, 4, 6)

b) Vodka Red bull. (1, 2, 4)

c) Wine. (1, 3, 4, 5, 6, 7)

d) Lots of water. (3, 5, 6, 7)

3. Once the sun sets:

a) Its going to be a party. (1, 2, 3, 4)

b) I'll unwind and relax. (3, 4, 5, 6, 7)

4. How will I spend each day?

a) Push it to the limit. I only have one gear, and it's full speed ahead. (1, 3, 6, 8)

b) Flop on a lounge chair like a blob of Jell-O. (6, 7)

c) Walk a lot. (5, 6, 7)

d) Keep active. (1, 2, 3)

5. My style is to:

a) Stay productive. (3)

b) Make an impression. (1, 2, 4, 8)

c) Live and let be. (6, 7)

d) Immerse myself. (5, 6)

6. When on vacation:

a) I spoil myself. After all, I deserve it. (1, 2, 4)

b) I refrain from overspending and going overboard. (3, 5, 6, 7)

7. I'm the type who:

a) Wants to know the quickest way from point A to B. (3)

b) Will be by the pool. (7)

c) Is curious to know what's around here. (5, 6)

d) Wants to see and be seen. (1, 2)

e) Seeks new, different, or exciting things. (4, 8)

8. My next trip will be:

a) A chance to do the things I cannot do at home. (5, 6)

b) Simple. I'll just soak in the moment. (7)

c) Awesome! (8)

d) A chance to live an alternate life for a few days. (1, 2, 4)

e) Well planned. (3)

9. I like to:

a) Go all out. (2, 8)

b) Make an impression. (1)

c) Keep busy. (3, 4)

d) Find peace and quiet. (6, 7)

e) Have balance. (5)

10. My suitcase will always have:

a) Casual clothes. (5, 6, 7)

b) Sharp attire. (1, 2, 3, 4)

c) Equipment and gear for adventures or excursions. (8)

11. I crave places that:

a) Are peaceful and quiet. (5, 6, 7)

b) Are tranquil, yet accessible to excitement. (1, 3, 4, 5)

c) Offer activities that I want to do over choosing a nice resort. (8)

d) Are in the center of the action. (2, 4)

12. When traveling, I seek:

a) To squeeze as much as I can out of my trip. (2, 8)

b) Balance. I take everything in moderation. (1, 3, 4, 5, 6)

c) Peace and quiet so I return relaxed and recharged. (3, 5, 6, 7)

13. On my next trip:

a) I will be out and about the entire time. (1, 2, 8)

b) I have a general list of things I might do. (5, 6, 7)

c) I know exactly what I'll be doing the entire time. (3)

d) I want to lose myself in the moment. (4, 8)

e) I'll decide what to do, once I'm there. (6, 7)

Calculate Your Score

To find your travel type, look up the numbers to the right of your answers and place a mark under the corresponding number, in the table below. For example, if your answer had the numbers (2, 4, 6) next to it, place a check mark under the numbers two, four, and six, and do the same for all your answers.

1	2	3	4	5	6	7	8

Interpreting the Results

Each number corresponds to the travel type with the corresponding number below. The one with most check marks is your dominant travel type.

Travel Types

1. Flash Packer

You are a real life macho man or a diva that's too hot to touch. You like to live large, are willing to jump at upgrades, and are likely to be found in swanky places, fancy restaurants, in VIP booths, and in the front row. You may be a jet setter or high roller (or want to be) and won't be found under-dressed for an occasion. You don't want to spend your weekend at the cabin; you're looking for places to see and be seen.

2. Wild One

You're a creature of the night and your wild side rises with the moon. You go where the action is and are out to have a great time and be with great people. You're like an Energizer bunny. Running on adrenaline is no problem for you, but sometimes you may overdo it. Is that you I saw in Ibiza? Or was it Vegas? No, I remember now. It was at the full moon party in Koh Phangan.

3. Traveler on a Mission

You've got things to do, and you have a plan to get them done. You like to mix pleasure with business, but lounging around the pool all day will bore you. You probably travel a fair bit, either for work, education, or conferences. You could be an expat, student, athlete, or performer. Chances are that some of your travels are either reimbursed by a company or organization or deductible for education, business, or through travel for a cause.

4. Escapist

You need a break away from your regular life every so often. Whether it's from the long winters or something that has you down, travel is a form of escapism for you to get what you don't have at home. Where you're going may not be as important as what you're getting away from.

5. Explorer

You want to see the world, experience authentic culture, and immerse yourself in your surroundings. You appreciate history, respect culture, and are curious. You're open-minded, genuine, welcoming, and sociable. You're up for new foods, sightseeing, and going on excursions. You're independent and able to navigate your way through stressful situations. You're looking for experiences that are different and want to travel to new places, not return to lands already conquered.

6. Rejuvenator

You travel to detach from whatever is that's draining you, as a way to keep your mind and spirit in balance. You can be at peace near home as much as afar, and you don't mind returning to the same destinations. You use your time away to step back, see the big picture, ponder different ways of addressing old problems, and to affirm your situation or decide to change it.

7. Tranquil Travel Bug

You travel to unwind, relax, and pamper yourself. You're content with simple pleasures and the company of close ones, and you avoid the craziness of the world. You find yourself at peace in tranquil settings, such as a rural cottage near a trickling creek. You share qualities with rejuvenators in that you need to occasionally escape to find solitude. You prefer to spend your days relaxing, reading, cooking, eating, lounging, and sightseeing.

8. Thrill Seeker

You're a bundle of energy! Traveling is a means to an adventure, and you get your thrills by pushing your comfort zone. You decide where to go based on what there is to do, be it extreme sports, adventure tours, activities, or new things to try.

If you only travel to places that flashy ads tell you to visit, I'll bet you the cost of your trip that you are spending *way* too much for far too little. By aligning your travels to your travel type, you can travel inexpensively and not have to skimp.

Want more? Try my favorite online surveys at breakthetravelbarrier.com under "TRAVEL TYPE."

6
Build Your Dream Travel Plan

It was a springtime Saturday night, and I was at my first pool party of the year. This was where I randomly walked into a conversation where the liveliest storyteller was describing his "out of this world" trip to Hong Kong. Listening to him had me so hyped up that I decided, on the spot, that my next trip would be to Hong Kong. The following day, I scoured websites for hours before realizing that Hong Kong would be a budget buster of a trip. What I didn't know at the time was that Hong Kong wasn't necessarily expensive to visit; the real problem was that I was going about it all wrong:

- I was looking in the wrong places and didn't know what the right places were.
- I was forcing dates without regard to peak and slow seasons.
- I had never thought of leveraging websites with loyalty programs, credit card benefits, and travel hospitality programs.

That's when I shut down my computer, sat back, and asked, "What are the odds the best deal to Hong Kong will fall precisely when I want to go? How likely is it that I am going to find the best deal on one of just five websites that I randomly used for my search?" I knew there had to be a better way …

That's when it hit me, and I said to myself, "Hong Kong isn't going anywhere Russ. There are other places I've wanted to visit for years that are a lot less expensive. Visit those places first, and buy the time to find a way to hack Hong Kong at a fraction of today's cost." I couldn't see how I would make it happen, but I could see the start line, and the rest unfolded exactly as you will soon read.

Getting Started

By planning differently, you can travel as much as anyone else on a fraction of what they pay. As you complete the following exercise, use the Dream Travel Planning form on page 87. A larger working version is also available at breakthetravelbarrier.com.

The key to stretching your travel budget is to pit all the places you want to visit against each other to compete for your next trip, then go with the least expensive option. As you start, keep in mind that the more options you have to choose from, the more you will be able to travel on less. That's why you should short list at least ten dream travel destinations that align to your travel type. Don't omit expensive destinations from your list, as I have visited many of these expensive cities on next to nothing, and the Dream Travel Plan will show you how to do so, as well.

Is Your Short List Too Short?

It amazes me how many people don't know what to do, once they break down the barriers holding them back. If you find yourself struggling to come up with at least ten places, jog some ideas by asking yourself, if time and money were no issue and you could travel anywhere, where would you go?

If you can't come up with ten destinations right away, give yourself time to percolate and look through some of the following magazines and websites to inspire you. Themes repeat themselves each year so you can save money on subscriptions by purchasing back issues that are less expensive, and you can get a stack of issues right away.

Inspiring Reads for All Travelers

- National Geographic Traveler and Conde Nast Traveler are loaded with exciting stories and suggestions for any travel type.
- Shermanstravel.com offers ideas, expert advice, and great deals.
- Get Lost is an Aussie magazine that inspires with adventure holiday suggestions and exciting stories.

For Thrifty Travelers

- budgettravel.com offers practical and timely tips and great deals. This is where I found a 4-day trip to Waikiki Beach for $500 including airfare, hotel and a luxury SUV rental.
- moneysavingexpert.com has a budget travel section titled "Travel Motoring."

For Knowledgeable Travelers

- Lonely Planet: The world's largest travel publisher floods off-beat destinations with thousands of visitors by merely mentioning them. They also have guidebooks on just about any place or travel subject you can think of.

- Frommer's: Since Arthur Frommer first wrote How to Travel Europe on $5 a Day in 1957, Frommer's has published hundreds of guidebooks and their website is a treasure trove of travel ideas, tips, tools, and chat forums.

For First-Class Travelers

- Travel and Leisure is a visual treat, featuring stunning locations and envious accommodations. The magazine touts savings upwards of 40% off at luxury hotels. Just remember that 40% off can still run you $200-$300 a night at hotels advertised next to ads by Rolex and Waldorf Astoria.

For Cultured Travelers

Afar magazine will inspire will an assortment of travel options by type of travel.

For Resourceful Travelers

Wanderlust is a leading publication for adventurous and authentic travel, and their website, wanderlust.co.uk is an archive of travel resources.

Niche Travel

campinglife.com features destinations, camping recipes, best vehicles, equipment, and the latest gear.

cruisetravelmag.com has the latest on new ships, the best cruise lines, most popular routes, and great deals.

trailerlife.com is great for RV travelers and those considering getting one.

Make Your Bucket List

Once you've short listed your top ten dream travel destinations, write them down in the Dream Travel Planning Form, below.

(Go to www.breakthetravelbarrier.com for a working size printable version.)

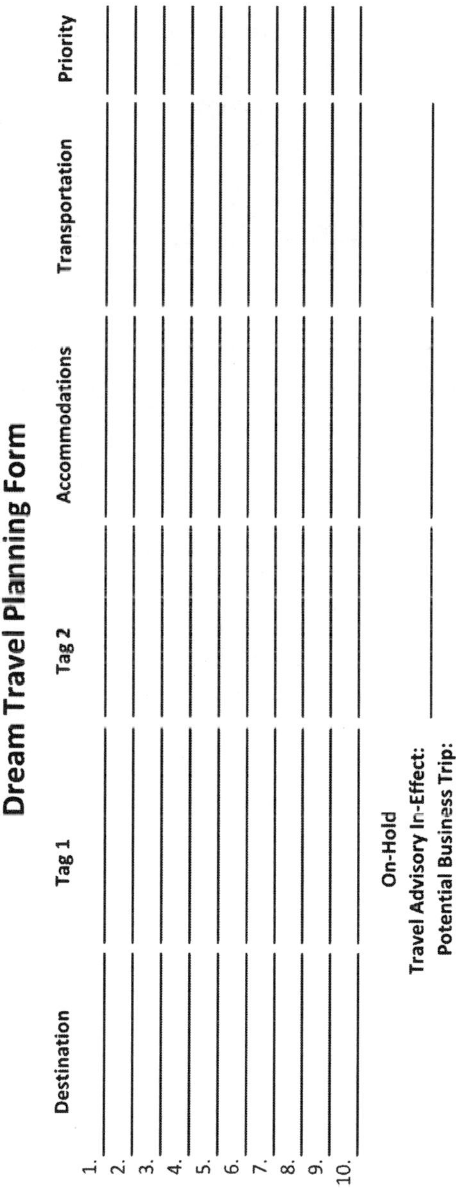

Dream Travel Planning Form

	Destination	Tag 1	Tag 2	Accommodations	Transportation	Priority
1.						
2.						
3.						
4.						
5.						
6.						
7.						
8.						
9.						
10.						

On-Hold

Travel Advisory In-Effect:

Potential Business Trip:

Anytime you may have an opportunity to visit one of your dream travel destinations on business, put that destination on-hold for personal travel. You do not want to waste limited means traveling to places you may get to visit for free. If your business trip materializes, plan your work week to start on a Monday or end on a Friday, and stay over the weekend on your own dime. If you cannot extend your stay, make the time to go out for lunch and to explore in the evenings. The same goes for out of town conferences and workshops. For more information on traveling on the company dime, go to page 113.

A Toast from the Top of the World

Perched high above the River Thames, our pod approached the pinnacle of the London Eye, and we pulled out two plastic cups and a miniature bottle of wine. "To another free trip!" No costs, fees, taxes, or surcharges. This trip was as free as free can be.

I had been dying to flee to Europe for months and was holding off because I had applied for a job and knew that, if I was selected, the company would fly me there for the interview. I figured there was no point in paying to go to London, until I knew that I had not been selected. I remember it like it was yesterday: My BlackBerry hummed to an email that said, "I have great news, company xyz would like to meet you for an interview and would like to fly you to London next week. Are you interested?" I thought, "This is too good to be true" and, once my flight was booked, I called the airline and postponed my return flight by four days. For the price of a change fee (ok so it wasn't 100% free), I spent five days in London riding double-decker buses, wandering Trafalgar Square, and catching shows in the West End with my British friends.

The lesson: Be selective so that you don't burn through limited means traveling to places you may one day be able to visit for free or for much less than it would cost to go today.

The first step most people take in planning their trip is usually the wrong one. It's where we decide to go and when. We want to go to the same places at the same times as everyone else, and that's why a hotel room that fetches $49 on Monday commands $350 on the weekend.

Travel Advisories

Destinations subject to travel advisories that pose a threat to your safety should be kept on hold until the advisory is lifted. Drug wars, hijackings, and violent civil disobedience aren't always covered in the news, and you want to know about them before you go. The U.S. Bureau of Consular Affairs' website travel.state.gov has a Smart Traveler Enrollment Program that educates travelers about potential risks abroad. The service is available to everyone, regardless of nationality, and issues e-mail alerts with advisory updates in areas you have requested updates for.

A friend of mine has been imploring me to visit her in Cairo and insisting that, despite the protests and political instability, there's nothing to worry about. Although I absolutely trust her judgement and believe I could very well visit without any problem, I have so many other low-risk options that it just makes smart sense to put Egypt on hold and reassess it in a few years.

Low-Cost Alternatives

Once you have short listed your dream travel destinations, you can travel more on the same budget by looking for comparable destinations in low-cost countries and adding them to your Dream Travel Plan. For example:

If You Like	Instead of	Consider
1. Spectacular natural scenery	Switzerland	South Africa
2. Proximity to geographical extremes	Lake Tahoe	Tanzania
3. Beaches	Caribbean	Southeast Asia

Next, maintain a traveler's mindset while at home, and do not overlook the wonders near home. Everywhere I go, I meet people who would rather spend time and money flying around the world without ever exploring the wonders in their backyards. People in cold climate countries crave palm trees and turquoise water in the dead of winter, whereas Californians dream of a white Christmas curled up by the fireplace, as they watch the snow fall outside. I have Hungarian friends who have never taken the four-hour drive to nearby Prague but fly to places like Hawaii and Asia every year. We fool ourselves into thinking that a thrill afar is greater than a thrill near home when, in truth, Prague is equally amazing whether you live five hours or five time zones away.

Sometimes we need to see things through the eyes of a tourist to appreciate the treasures near home. This happened to me when Lee Abbamonte—the youngest American to visit every country in the world—proclaimed in an interview that Calgary is the number one place he recommends for a nearby international escape. He described at length how the views from Lake Louise to Jasper were amongst the most beautiful he had ever seen and that the people were the nicest he had ever met.

In the words of Dagobert D. Runes, "People travel to faraway places to watch, in fascination, the kind of people they ignore at home." By keeping a traveler's mindset, we are more likely to take full advantage of the wonders near home.

Prioritize Your Dream Travel Destinations

Your wants and needs will vary from trip to trip. Whether it's to decompress, let loose, have a girl's getaway, or take a family vacation, make a list of all the reasons you travel and tag those reasons to the destinations that meet those needs under the "Tag" column in the Dream Travel Planning Form. For example:

- If you take family vacations every summer, tag "family" to each family friendly destination on your list.
- If you take winter escapes each year, tag "winter escape" to the tropical destinations on your list.

The most commonly used travel tags include: Adventure, Explore, Friends, Family Vacation, Guys Weekend, Girls Getaway, Let Loose, Relax, and Winter Escapes.

If your travel objective is to:		Consider:
1	Break from your routine	The least expensive destinations on your list.
2	See a place (as opposed to an event)	Go when it's most affordable. For instance, avoid Vatican City during conclave.
3	Escape the cold	Ignore deals for 40% off to Cancun in July.
4	Immerse in to local culture	Don't stay in an all-inclusive resort.

Try not to assign a travel tag to too many destinations so that you can filter your Dream Travel Plan based on the type of trip you want to take.

Now that you have tagged your Dream Travel destinations, select the destinations with tags that resonate with the next trip you want to take, then sort them from least to most expensive to visit. Your least expensive option is where you should take your next trip.

Sorting your destinations from least to most expensive can get confusing, and the following scale will help you get through this exercise. Keep in mind, this scale is best applied for trips of two or more weeks:

All Other Things Being Equal:				
Prioritize	1	Short Window of Opportunity	OVER	Available Anytime
	2	Truly Free Accommodations		Free Accommodations by redeeming non-financial means
	3	Options you can fund with non-financial means		Options requiring you to pay out of pocket
	4	Accommodations with kitchens		Accommodations requiring you to eat out every meal
	5	Free Accommodations		Free Transportation
*If two destinations are tied on your short list, go with your favorite option				

Assuming all other things are equal, the above chart is telling you:

Row 1: Prioritize opportunities with a finite window over places you can visit anytime. That means if you have a sibling studying abroad for a term, go while you can.

Row 2: Prioritize places where you have a free place to stay over others that require you to redeem limited non-financial means, such as rewards points, coupons, or vouchers.

Row 3: Prioritize options where you can pay with non-financial means (such as rewards points, voluntourism, house sitting, or home swapping) over others requiring you to pay out of pocket.

Row 4: Prioritize accommodations with kitchens over others that don't so that you don't have to eat out three times a day. The same goes with hotels, prioritize ones that offer complimentary continental breakfasts over others that don't.

Row 5: Accommodations are generally your highest expense for trips of two weeks or more. In these cases, prioritize options where you have a free place to stay over others where you may have free transportation but have to pay for accommodations.

Since accommodations are generally your largest travel expense, prioritize options where you have free and inexpensive places to stay.

There are two types of **free accommodations**:

i. No strings attached

ii. Available with limited non-financial means, such as rewards points

The game is to start with destinations where you have truly free, no-strings-attached accommodations. Once you have exhausted those options, move down your list to destinations where you can get free accommodations using non-financial means. To do this in the Dream Travel Planning Form, go to the "Accommodations" column and:

1. Write "Free Stays" next to each destination where you have a free place to stay. These are automatically at the top of your list of places to visit first.

2. Tag destinations where you can get free accommodations by redeeming non-financial means. Specify in the "Accommodations" column what you need to redeem.

3. Continue on until each destination indicates your accommodation options with a cost estimate.

4. Under the "Transportation" column, indicate the mode of transportation you will use to get there, along with a cost estimate so you can compare the relative cost of each option.

Quality over Quantity

Instead of visiting five temples a day, every day, find the mother of all temples and go to that one first. See the best there is, right away, then move on to other things.

Once finished, your Dream Travel Plan should look like this:

Rank Destination	Tag 1	Tag 2	Accommodations	Transportation
1. South Beach	Friends	Party	Lisa's place	Jenn's buddy pass (Flight Attendant)
2. San Francisco	Friends	Sports	Adam's place	Car, 5 hour drive
3. Melbourne	Winter Escape	Explore	Hotel rewards	Flight rewards points
4. Geneva	Explore	Adventure	Camping	Flight ($680) or car rental ($560)

Maintain Your Dream Travel Plan

As with any plan, you need to maintain your Dream Travel Plan and update it to reflect your changing tastes, lifestyle, and costs of travel. You also should re-assess your Dream Travel Plan anytime you have a major life change, such as a move to a new city, a new relationship, having kids, or becoming an empty nester.

7

Food — Eat Well on Your Home Grocery Budget

If you eat out three times a day, you will spend five times more than your at-home grocery bill, on average. The most influential factor affecting your cost of eating is whether you are staying in grocery friendly accommodations. Of course, you aren't going to choose your accommodations strictly on this. But it is important to consider food friendliness when comparing your options.

QUIZ

How would you rank the following options from most (1) to least (5) food friendly?

Rank

a. _____ Hotel with an in-room refrigerator

b. _____ Hotels and bed & breakfasts that offer continental breakfasts

c. _____ Fully furnished apartment with a kitchen

d. _____ All-inclusive resort

e. _____ Standard hotel room with no refrigerator

Answers

Here is how I rank the options, in terms of food friendliness:

The winner: D

All-inclusive packages cover your food and accommodations, but keep in mind that terms vary by resort so make sure to ask whether gratuities and alcohol are included. If not, always assume that alcohol will cost a premium, and ask whether gratuities are fixed at a set daily rate.

Second: C

Fully furnished apartments with kitchens offer all the amenities of home, making it easy to keep your cost of eating on par with your usual grocery bill.

Third: B

The next best options are hotels that offer free continental breakfasts. Continental breakfasts are convenient and cut the cost of your first meal of the day. By leveraging continental breakfasts with the following tips and tricks, you can eat well on $10 a day.

Confessions of an Ultra-Economical Eater

When I stay in hotels that offer continental breakfasts, I eat just before breakfast ends, which is around 10 o'clock, and I pack a banana and bagel to snack on throughout the day. When I do this, my appetite usually picks up just before 4 o'clock which is when most lunch specials end. By catching a lunch special at the last minute, I can have a soup and sandwich or pasta and salad for $9 to $12, and that's the only meal I pay for all day. To save an additional 22% off my already inexpensive lunch, I eat at restaurants that sell gift cards at Costco, which sells $100 gift cards for $80. On top of that, executive Costco members are entitled to an additional 2% off all Costco purchases. I use these gift cards to pay for my lunch specials, and the savings from the gift cards alone largely covers the tax and tip.

Fourth: A

Many hotel rooms come with refrigerators and/or microwaves at no extra charge. As a rule, I always ask for a room that has these appliances, under the condition that there is no additional charge.

By making the following tweaks to your grocery list, you can eat healthily and inexpensively in a hotel room.

i. Stick to foods that do not need to be chopped or cooked.

ii. If you don't have a microwave, stick to cold meals.

iii. If you don't have a refrigerator, buy:

- Fruits that do not need to be refrigerated such as bananas, kiwis, and pears.
- Dried fruit, nuts, cereal, granola, crackers, bagels, baguettes, and peanut butter.

- Soy milk, water, and one refrigerated meal that you can eat shortly after doing your groceries.
- To preserve groceries requiring refrigeration, hotels always have ice machines so just put the groceries on ice in your sink, bathtub, or ice bucket.

TIP

Always ask for a room with a refrigerator and microwave at no extra charge. This works for me about one out of every three times.

Least Food Friendly Accommodation: E

Standard hotel rooms that have neither a refrigerator nor a microwave are your least "food friendly" options. That said, you can still get by on the grocery list just provided.

Ultra-Economical Eating Tips

- If you use groupon.com or livingsocial.com for e-coupons, change your home city to your vacation destination before your next trip to get newsletters with coupons offering upwards of 40% off on restaurants, hotels, spas, golf, and excursions.
- Farmers markets offer authentic and relatively inexpensive excursions.
- When flying, pack snacks to avoid pricey airport and airline concessions.
- On road trips, bring a cooler packed with the sorts of food you would typically have for lunch at work.
- Unprepared foods require facilities and time to prepare but are generally healthier and inexpensive.

- Hotel restaurants generally charge more for the convenience.
- Fine dining restaurants charge for the ambience. Instead of having dinner, stop in for a drink and eat elsewhere.

Did You Know ...

Some airports, such as Vienna International Airport, have grocery stores in the terminal where you can get groceries at prices comparable to local grocery stores.

Tipping

You might be surprised to learn how many places in the world do not want or expect tips for service. You are actually following custom by not tipping in much of Australia, New Zealand, Scandinavia, Iceland, parts of Europe, the Middle East, China, and Southeast Asia. Don't even think about tipping in Japan, as the Japanese feel insulted by the offer of a tip.

How Much to Tip

Tipping gets confusing in countries that expect tips for certain services (like taxis) but not for others (like restaurants). If you are ever unsure:

- Tipulator is an application (app) that tells you how much to tip by location.
- Ask locals or peek to see how much the person next to you is tipping.

Rules of Thumb

- North America and Commonwealth countries: Tip 15% (except for the U.K., Australia, and New Zealand).
- Asia and the U.K.: Don't tip.
- Everywhere else, tip 10% except for:
    - Porters: Tip $1/bag.
    - Taxis:
        - For fares under $20, round your tip up to the next dollar plus $1.
        - For fares over $20, tip 10-15% .

Despite your best intentions, you're going to make an occasional mistake and, if that's the biggest mistake you make on the road, you'll be doing just fine.

If you find yourself unable to tip ...

Go out of your way to tell your server how much you appreciate his or her service and that you want to leave a tip but can't and feel bad about it. Any decent person will appreciate your compliment and sincerity.

A few years back, I had a rude bartender in Whistler and chose not to tip her. She glaringly pointed out that I forgot to give her something (further speaking to her rudeness) so I explained I did not tip her because of a few things she said to me. That brought out her true colors, and she stood up on the bar, pointed at me, and called out to everyone in the restaurant that I was a cheap guy who wouldn't tip her. Ouch! It's too bad because I otherwise really liked the place.

8
Accommodations

"Spend the night not a fortune"
– Hotel sign near Fundy National Park in Canada

Free Accommodations

Hotels are as expensive as they have ever been. At the same time, there have never been more free and inexpensive alternative accommodations to choose from. As we covered earlier, there are two types of free accommodations:

1. Truly free no-strings-attached accommodations, such as staying with friends and family and travel hospitality.
2. Accommodations acquired through non-financial means, such as rewards points, bonus nights, home swapping, house sitting, and voluntourism.

1. Truly free accommodations come mostly from the people passport and, to a lesser extent, from being flexible. They include:

I. Friends and Family

II. Travel Hospitality

III. Home Swapping

IV. House Sitting

V. Overnight Trips

VI. Camping Wagons and Sleep Friendly Vehicles

I. Friends and Family

For the second time, I was putting off a trip to Greece. And for the second time, it was because I could visit an equally amazing place at a fraction of the cost. The first was Monaco; this time, I was going to Vienna. In both cases, I pretty much had free accommodations and, as heart wrenching as it was to put off Greece yet again, I realized that, while Greece will always be there, the opportunity to visit my mother in Vienna wouldn't be. Moms are always right, and my trip to Vienna turned out to be one of the all-time great trips of my life.

Your top priority should be to visit places where you have friends and family to stay with. By holding off on destinations where you don't know anyone, in favor of ones where you do, you buy yourself the time to expand your network and, over time, you are likely to make friendships with people who live in the places you want to visit. By inviting friends to visit, you are opening the door for them to reciprocate.

II. Travel Hospitality

Many travelers and sociable people enjoy hosting travelers, while at home, and this is an ultra-economical option for those who are open-minded, adaptable, and sociable. Travel hospitality websites connect hosts with travelers looking for a free place to stay and are becoming a mainstream alternative to hotels.

"Why Would Someone Host Strangers For Free?"

Travel hosts are often travelers themselves, who are sociable and like-minded people who simply enjoy showcasing their hometown and connecting with other travelers.

Planning Your First Travel Hospitality Stay

Stick to travel hospitality websites that charge membership fees. Free websites are prone to have more scammers and suspect characters.

The host is always in the driver's seat but, whether you're a host or a guest, it is important to get to know the other before committing to a visit, especially if you will be sharing the same living space. To screen others:

1. Review their profile and reviews posted by others on the website.
2. Discuss the house rules.
3. Invite the person to a Skype call and to connect on social media.
4. If you are the host, target travelers who live in places you want to visit, and ask if they would consider one day hosting you.

If something doesn't feel right, simply say you will follow up tomorrow then inform the person in writing that your circumstances changed. If it goes well, set up a second, third, fourth call etc., until you are both comfortable and ready to move forward.

Etiquette

Travel hospitality is best used for short stays of a week or less. As a guest, always reciprocate to your hosts, either by paying for excursions they take with you, taking them out for dinner, cooking, offering a gift, or helping in any way you can.

Travel Hospitality Resources

Travel hospitality originated after World Word War II, when Bob Luitweiler envisioned the healing hatred and wounds of war by giving youth the opportunity to travel and stay in homes with foreign families. As part of this peace movement, Servas was founded, a multicultural hospitality association with a network of hosts in over 100 countries who open their doors to young travelers.

Travel hospitality networks have since flourished, especially with the advent of the internet. They include:

couchsurfing.com

globalfreeloaders.com

hospitalityclub.org

homestay.com

homestayclub.com

homestayfinder.com

servas.org

worldwidehomestay.com

III. Home Swapping

Did you know your home can earn you free accommodations on your next trip? Home swapping (or home exchanges) is exchanging your place with others, and it's an increasingly popular way to get free, fully furnished accommodations while traveling. It's an especially great option for young families who can swap homes with other families with the same number of children in the same age range. This way, your vacation home will have the right number of bedrooms and anything you need from cribs, strollers, and toys. In fact, you can even swap homes with families near home, just for a change of pace.

For home swapping to be a viable option, be ready to put your flexibility and adaptability passports to work, as it isn't easy to find fellow home swappers who:

1. Live where you want to go AND who want to stay at your place.
2. Are available to swap at the same time as you.

Make Your Home Swappable

Smoking is often a deal breaker and pets can be, as well, to those who do not have any. Everyone might not be as fond of your 1970s wallpaper as you are. To improve your chances of finding someone to swap homes with, look for fellow home swappers with homes and lifestyles that are comparable to yours.

The Talk

In the home swapping game, structure trumps spontaneity. No matter how courteous others are, you cannot expect them to understand your expectations unless you specifically tell them. To prevent undesirable things from happening, be forthright with your guests about what they can and cannot do, secure your valuables, lock areas you do not want them to access, and ask what house rules they have for you.

Paperwork

To prevent misunderstandings, ask your fellow home swappers to write their expectations for you and do the same for them. Many home exchange websites offer templates that you can use as contracts.

Etiquette

Leave your house guests a warm welcome letter with information on where to find things and any nearby shops or stores you recommend. Include a gentle reminder of any house rules, and wish them a wonderful stay.

Insurance – When Things Go Wrong

To insurance companies, home swapping is the equivalent of lending your car. Any damage to your home is generally covered under home and renter's insurance, so long as your house guests are not paying you to stay there. However, the moment money is exchanged, it becomes a business arrangement and homeowner and rental insurance will not cover you. Terms and conditions can vary by policy so always check with your insurance company to understand the specific terms and conditions of your policy.

Home Swapping Websites[3]

homeexchange.com was featured in the movie "The Holiday" and is one of the largest and best known home exchange service in the world.

homeforswap.com is a European home exchange website with listings in over 120 countries. It is available in six languages and has handy tools.

thevacationexchange.com has a unique twist to traditional home swapping. People offer their empty place or vacation home to others, in exchange for credits they can later redeem to stay in accommodations offered through the vacation exchange network. This service has a higher match rate than traditional home swapping websites, as it eliminates the need to find someone to swap with.

IV. House Sitting

There are people all over the world looking for trustworthy and reliable house keepers to maintain their homes and care for their pets while they are away. If you have experience as a professional housekeeper or maid, you have an advantage over others who don't, and you should be taking full advantage by house sitting to offset your travel costs.

House sitting is going to require you to use your adaptability passport. If you are fixated on house sitting in Nantucket during the summer, you are likely to end up disappointed.

House Sitting Websites:

caretaker.org (Subscribe to caretaker ads)

housecarers.com

housesit.org

housesitmatch.com (Australia and U.K.)

luxuryhousesitting.com

mindmyhouse.com

trustedhousesitters.com

V. Overnight Trips

Philadelphia, September 9th, 2014: It was the night before a workshop. Hundreds of authors were visiting from all over and were readying for bed. I was doing the same, only instead of being in a hotel room, I was getting ready to sleep on a red eye from San Francisco. I slept on the plane, landed at 7 a.m., and my hotel allowed me to check in at 7:30 a.m., at no extra charge. I was able to freshen up and make it to the workshop right on time.

If you are blessed with the ability to sleep while on a plane, train, or automobile, you can save yourself the cost of a night's accommodations by scheduling long haul travel overnight. When I do this and don't sleep as well as I expected, I inexpensively catch up on my sleep when I arrive at my destination, either by visiting a spa with a nap room or finding a discounted hotel rooms at daytime-only rates at bookadayroom.com.

VI. Camping Wagons and Sleep Friendly Vehicles

My vacations as a kid were camping trips to the island in the family camping van. It had a kitchenette and dining table that folded into a bed, and we brought a tent that my brother and I slept in. You can often justify the added cost of getting a sleep friendly vehicle, based on what it can save you on travel accommodations. The Volkswagen Caddy Tramper is an example of a van that has everything you need while on the road, except a toilet. Sport utility vehicles and crossovers often have a big enough back to lay out a foam or air mattress and can be used in tandem with a tent. Here are some important vehicle accessories you will want to have, if you will be sleeping in your vehicle:

- Tinted rear windows
- Sun shades for extra privacy at night and shade in the morning
- A sunroof you can leave slightly open for fresh air
- A rooftop cargo box for your luggage

If you don't want to pay for a camping lot, consider pulling over for the night in campground parking lots, places where your vehicle blends in and where you are close to a restroom. Parking lots for big hotels work well, as the people at the reception desk will not be suspicious if you go to the lobby washroom in the middle of the night. You can also opt for parking lots of stores that are open 24/7 such as certain Wal-Marts. Another option for guys (especially if you're an off duty truck driver) is truck stops, as they offer all the amenities and conveniences you need at night and to freshen up in the morning. Just remember that truck stops are for professional truckers. Rigs are big, loud, and come and go at all hours of the night so this option is best when it's late and you just need a few hours' sleep. Stay away from the truck parking area and bring earplugs.

Don't do this if:

- Anything makes you feel uncomfortable. If something doesn't feel right, trust your gut and find a room.
- You cannot sleep at a comfortable temperature with the engine off.

Remember, we want to be ultra-economical and not cheap. Don't expose yourself to vulnerable situations.

Free Accommodations Using Non-Financial Means

There are four main types of non-financial means you can leverage to get free travel accommodations:

I. Group Travel Tours

II. Voluntourism

III. Rewards Programs

IV. Traveling on the Company Dime

I. Group Travel Tours

If you are in college or have a talent for rallying people together, you can earn free trips as an affiliate group travel operator. All you need to do is:

1. Contact a group tour operator and ask how many people you would need to sign up to a tour to earn yourself a free spot. You can try this with the following group travel operators:

   gadventures.com

   go-today.com

   freeandeasytraveler.com

   Intrepid Travel

2. If you are a student, a great way to get a free trip for spring break or a grad trip is to run an on-campus campaign. Affix posters all over campus, invite your teammates, tell everyone in residence, and buy the campus DJ drinks to plug your trip. The people you recruit will thank you for organizing the trip and never know that you got to go for free.

II. Voluntourism

If there are a million ways to make a living, there are just as many ways you can travel through voluntourism. It's common for professionals, such as dental hygienists and tradespeople, to voluntour, but you don't need to have special skills. Farmers will teach you how to milk cows and forest rangers will show you how to plant trees and repair hiking trails. The following websites will help you find voluntour opportunities that are right for you:

Calling All Hikers:

Repair hiking trails in the U.S. in exchange for free room and board:

americanhiking.org

continentaldividetrail.org

World Wide Opportunities on Organic Farms

Although most farms offer accommodations in exchange for work, some farms offer pay. How it works is that you sign up with WWOOF for a fee (fees varies from country to country), and you receive a booklet detailing WWOOF hosts by area, along with a description of what farmers are looking for.

wwoofinternational.org

wwoof.org

More Voluntourism Websites

caretaker.org

globalvolunteers.org

goabroad.com

helpx.net

idealist.org

podvolunteer.org

rotary.org

unitedplanet.org

III. Loyalty Programs

When planning a trip on rewards points, seek out options that require the fewest points to be redeemed. If you missed the section on rewards programs and loyalty points, you will find it on page 44.

IV. Traveling on the Company Dime

It started just like every other Monday morning at the office. My software consultant had just walked in the door and was visiting from Boston. Her name was Shelley, and I asked, during our coffee break, what her impression was of Calgary. Her enthusiastic response suggested that she was hoping I would ask. Shelley explained that she arrived Friday night and spent the weekend exploring the mountains; she was awestruck by the magnificence of the Canadian Rockies. She went on to share that her work has her traveling 90% of the time, and she routinely extends her business trips through weekends, to explore the places she is visiting on her own dime.

At lunch, I brought Shelley to a local market and brought up the subject again, which was when Shelley told me she spent the previous week in Tokyo and her clients took her to a pier for fresh sushi. The following week, she was going to London. By the time we finished our lunch, I had learned two things:

1. Cats are the only suitable pets for globetrotters like Shelley (whose cats no longer recognize her).

2. Shelley's job afforded her a travel lifestyle and not only while traveling on business. By charging her travel expenses to her personal credit card and later claiming those expenses to her company, Shelley stockpiles enough points to cover all her personal vacations and still has enough points left over to bring an occasional guest with her.

   In cases where her clients pay her travel expenses, loyalty programs award points to the guest or ticketholder, regardless of who paid. So, in these cases, Shelley is still earning rewards points. For more information on how to leverage business travel to earn more rewards points, visit page 44.

Shelley's story illustrates how business travelers have access to a travel lifestyle that might not otherwise be affordable. Having worked with a number of public companies, business travel has taken me to just about every corner of North America. I also have colleagues who have had international assignments in Poland, Singapore, Beijing, Melbourne, Doha, Abu Dhabi, Ankara, and Anchorage, just to name a few.

Military Travel Benefits

When we think of companies with the most generous travel benefits, airlines are the first that come to mind. But there many other industries that offer generous travel benefits including military personnel and their families, who qualify for free or deeply discounted accommodations on bases and nearby hotels that cater to the military and visitors. Volunteers and part-time reserves are sometimes also entitled to these perks, which vary by country and branch of service, but can include:

- A travel per diem.
- Access to ride on military planes on personal time (pending availability).
- Access to military accommodations at military rates.
- A slew of military travel discounts and preferential treatment.

Corporate Rates

Corporate rates generally entitle you to:

- 10-15% off posted rates.
- Flexible itineraries and reasonably priced change fees.
- Unlimited mileage and car rentals.

If you work for a company that has negotiated corporate rates, never pay any more than the rate while traveling.

Paid Accommodations

Three things influence the cost of travel:

I. Currency differentials

II. Local cost of living

III. Knowing where and how to get the best price

I. Currency Differentials

If you are from Kuwait, congratulations, you are the world's currency king, and you command a currency advantage anywhere you travel. But, if you're from Zimbabwe, you will need to rely on the travel passports more than anyone else. Before the Zimbabwe dollar was suspended, your travel bill would have terrified you as a $100 trillion bill was worth about $5 U.S. dollars.

For everyone else in between, leverage the following strategies the best you can, relative to the value of your national currency.

If you live in a strong currency country:

Having a currency advantage over a country you are visiting equates to money in your pocket. It makes such a difference that you can live for years in Southeast Asia on what would only last you a few months in the U.S. That's why destinations in weak currency countries should rank higher on your priority list than others with strong currencies.

When you find yourself visiting multiple countries with different currencies, get the most out of your dollar by minimizing expenses in high currency countries, in favor of those with lower currency valuations. For example, if you're on your way to Croatia, you can stop for the night, fuel up, and load up on supplies in Slovenia, at a fraction of what it costs in Croatia.

If you live in a weak currency country:

i. Seek to visit countries with weaker currencies than your own.

ii. The travel passports and Dream Travel Plan can help you overcome your currency handicap.

II. Cost Of Living

Having a currency advantage does not necessarily translate into an inexpensive vacation. Let's say you have a currency advantage over the Japanese yen so you decide to spend two weeks in Tokyo. It just so happens that Tokyo is one of the world's most expensive cities, and the cost of living is likely to more than offset your currency advantage.

To find the relative cost of living of your Dream Travel destinations, use the numbeo.com cost-of-living index or run a Google search for "Mercer cost of living full list."

III. Get the Best Price for Accommodations

To quickly find the best and least expensive accommodations for you, refer to the list of paid travel accommodations below, which are sorted from least-to-most expensive. For example, camping is ranked as number one because it is generally the least expensive form of paid accommodations. On the other hand, hotels are at the bottom of the list because they are generally the most expensive option. Just start at the top of the list and work your way down. By searching this way, the first option you find that suits you is likely to also be your most economical one.

Types of Paid Accommodations

1. Camping
2. Timeshare Presentations
3. Private Rentals
4. Hostels
5. University Dorms (May through August)
6. Bed & Breakfasts
7. Hotels/Resorts

1. Camping

Although you can set up camp in many places for free, I recommend sticking to professionally run campgrounds as they offer security, toilets, showers, and safety from wildlife. You can stay at many campsites for as little as $15 and between $25 and $35 per night, on average.

Campingcheque.com gives you access to more than 640 campsites in 29 countries for 16 Euros a night. You can use the following national campground directories to find campgrounds in:

- Australia: camping.com.au
- Canada: camping-canada.com
- Europe:

  campingeurope.com

  eurocampings.co.uk

  europe-camping-holiday.com

  camping.info
- New Zealand: tourism.net.nz
- U.S. & Canada: uscampgrounds.info

If you opt to use a camper instead of a tent, make sure to factor in the added fuel costs and get one with a kitchenette to cut your costs of eating.

Recreational Vehicles (RV's)

RVing isn't just a way to travel, it's a way of life. To many people, their RV is their home on wheels.

Financial Considerations:

- Big fuel bills. Before you buy, estimate how much driving you will do, find out what gas mileage your RV will get, and forecast your fuel costs.
- Lot fees and utility hook-up charges add up. Try occasionally staying at rest stops and Wal-Mart parking lots, to keep these fees at bay. Wal-Mart encourages RV owners to park overnight, knowing they are also likely shoppers.

Before You Buy a Camper or RV

- If you know anyone who has an RV, ask if they would rent it to you. RVs spend much of the year parked, and owners often wouldn't mind the extra income.
- Consider buying used.
- Split the cost of an RV with friends or family and share it.

2. Timeshare Presentations

Sixty minutes of your time can land you two nights in a fully furnished luxury condo, for the price of a hostel. The catch? You will be asked to attend an ownership sales presentation.

Orlando, Florida, is proclaimed as the "vacation capital of the world" and has enough vacation properties to populate a small city. Many of these vacation properties are funded through timeshare ownership. The way timeshares work is that people purchase a title and contribute to the maintenance costs of a pool of vacation resorts, entitling them to spend a set number of nights each year at any of the resorts in the network.

Timeshare operators know that the more wealthy vacationers they pitch, the more timeshare ownership packages they can sell. They do this by enticing vacationers to visit, offering their most valuable asset—bargain accommodations—in exchange for attending a no-obligation presentation about ownership opportunities. It's also common for timeshare resorts to offer additional incentives, such as vouchers for food and entertainment, DVD players, event tickets, and even cash.

I attend at least one timeshare sales presentation every year and have stayed in fully furnished condos more than a dozen times. It's so easy to do, there is no reason why you cannot do the same. Many of the timeshare invitations I get come from attending travel shows, where exhibitors draw prizes for attendees who provide their contact information. I sign up to all contests offered by timeshare companies and, although I have never won the advertised prize, I always receive a call a few days later for an invitation to visit their resort at a discounted rate, as long as I agree to attend a no-obligation timeshare sales presentation during my stay.

Travel shows are not the only place to get invitations to timeshare sales pitches. If you call their sales office and say you are looking to buy a timeshare, the agent will ask what your household income is and whether all decision makers can attend. If you meet their criteria, you will be on your way to getting a discounted, fully furnished apartment.

Timeshare Resorts

Intervalworld.com has an online directory of vacation ownership operators worldwide.

U.S. Resorts

hiltongrandvacations.com

orangelake.com

westgateresorts.com

Worldwide

clubintrawest.com

diamondresorts.com

hyattresidenceclub.com

rci.com

shellvacationsclub.com

wyndhamvacationresorts.com

Surviving a Timeshare Sales Pitch

When you arrive for your timeshare presentation, you will be greeted with snacks, juice, and coffee. You will likely get to watch a tantalizing video and receive brochures on how timeshare ownership can get you the travel lifestyle you always wanted. Then comes the sales pitch.

If you have no intention of purchasing, every minute you stay above and beyond the minimum, agreed upon time commitment adds to your non-financial cost of staying there. When they apply high pressure sales tactics, call them on it. Firmly say you cannot afford it and that they are in no position to tell you what you should do with your money. Then, say thanks, and get out.

Tips and Tricks

i. If you're traveling with someone else, you can double up on the duration of your timeshare stay by booking separate stays back-to-back.

ii. Ambitious travel hackers can spend weeks in resort towns skipping from one timeshare resort to another by signing up to as many timeshare sales presentations as they can and having their travel companions do the same on successive nights.

3. Private Rentals

Your most economical option for trips of two weeks or more is to opt for shared accommodations and private rentals that target locals. This way, you can get all the conveniences and amenities you have at home, at prices that locals pay.

If you're sociable and easygoing, shared accommodations are less expensive than private rentals and can be more fulfilling, as you will get to know the people you are staying with. Before you commit, invest the time up front to speak with the people you will be staying with, just as you would with travel hospitality, to get a sense of whether you are compatible.

The best place to find shared and private rentals is in online classifieds that target locals. I also recommend the following websites, knowing these options will be more expensive than what you will find in local classifieds:

airbnb.com offers private and shared accommodations.

homeaway.com has more than 625,000 listings worldwide.

stayrentals.com specializes in private accommodations in Europe.

transitionsabroad.com offers a directory of accommodations by location.

vrbo.com (Vacation Rentals by Owner) posts fully furnished homes and condos.

wimdu.com posts private accommodations for significantly less than the price of hotels.

4. Hostels

If you are simply looking for a good night's sleep, hostels offer communal accommodations and a budget alternative to hotels. Although some hostels offer private rooms, always go in with the expectation that you will be sharing a room and that washrooms and showers will be communal. Anything more is a bonus.

Hostels are popular with younger travelers, and you are sure to meet people from all over the world. If you are traveling as a group, contact a hostel before your trip to see if you can reserve an entire room for your group.

Just like buying a car, you have to assess each hostel on its own merits. Most hostels offer basic accommodations with shared facilities but, if you do your research, you can find hostels that rival upscale hotels with impressive design, quality linens, free Wi-Fi, and complimentary continental breakfasts.

Keep in Mind:

- Some hostels have age restrictions and curfews. Policies vary by hostel so check their website before you go.

- Occasionally, you are bound to get a bunk mate who is not as considerate as you. My friend once walked into his room to find someone drying his dirty shoes and socks with a blow dryer.

Worldwide Hostel Directories

hostelbookers.com is an independent international hostel booking website that does not charge booking fees.

hostelworld.com has a GPS-integrated app so you can find hostels nearest you.

Tokyo on $50 a Night

Unless you are claustrophobic, the Capsule hotel is the best priced hotel in Tokyo. For $50, you get a sleeping capsule that could be mistaken for the hypersleep pods you see in space movies. The elevator and toilet are no larger, making it likely you will hit your head on the door as you sit. There is no storage space for luggage, but you do get a locker big enough for your shoes, clothes, and purse.

5. University Dorms

With college dormitories largely abandoned for the summer, many rent out rooms to the general public during summer break. Just think of all the opportunities that open up, when you visit places that have colleges in their city center:

- London University offers summer bed & breakfast packages for as little as 35 Pounds/night.
- Venice International University is on the island of San Servolo and is just a 10 minute boat ride to Venice's historical center.

College dormitories generally offer rooms with one or two beds and have communal washroom facilities, coin operated laundry machines, and pay phones. If you are traveling during the summer, look up the colleges and universities in that area, and contact their on-campus accommodation services to find out if they rent rooms during summer.

6. Bed & Breakfasts

With bed & breakfasts, you get a bedroom in someone's home and are served breakfast in the morning. Ireland and Scotland are legendary for their bed & breakfasts, and you are also likely to find them in small towns that do not have hotels. They were once part of the experience of visiting New York City, until the city cracked down with tough legislation targeting people who were illegally sub-dividing homes and running them like hotels.

Websites

bedandbreakfast.com has a worldwide directory of bed & breakfasts, organized by travel interest, and offers deals in their weekly newsletter.

bedandbreakfastworld.com lists for more than 26,000 bed & breakfasts worldwide.

7. Hotels and Resorts

Hotels and resorts are your most expensive options for lodging and are, therefore, your "resort of last resort." The advertised price is only part of the problem. Hotels set the standard at masking true cost (airlines come in at a close second) and thrive on surcharges and questionable "taxes" that add up to more than $2 billion a year.[4]

The Hidden Cost of Hotels

– Guest fee after 11 p.m.	Half the cost of the room
– Snacks	$12 per bag of cashews, $10 for bottled water
– Snack replenishment	$6 to refill your basket with more cashews
– Reservation changes	Amounts vary by booking and operator
– No cancellation/transfer policies	Total value of your booking
– Deliver something to your room	$5
– Internet	$30 per day
– Business center charges	Some places charge fees for anything you do
– Parking (valet / self-park)	$50 per day
– Futon	$35
– Daily towel replenishment	$5 per day
– Elevator access fee	One penny per ride
– Housekeeping fee	$23 per day (Atlantis, Bahamas)
– Resort fee	$30 per day (or more)
– Luggage stowage	$5
– Utility costs	$85 per day, per person
– Early check-in / late checkout	$50
– Fees to pay with credit card	1.5%
– In-room safe	$1 – 3 per day
– Energy surcharges	$12 per day
– Horse stabling fee	Even if you don't have a horse!
– Table decorations	$30
– Pre-authorization	Up to $1,000 – Leaving you vulnerable
– Gym drop-in fee	$40 / workout
– Phone calls	$15 for the first minute and $1 / minute thereafter
– Early check-in	Varies
– Late check-out	Varies

What may appear to be courtesy services could, in fact, be costly. To be safe:

1. Ask, up front, whether all costs have been disclosed to you, and get written confirmation.

2. Ask, up front, whether there is a charge for a service being offered.

3. Review your bills and invoices closely, to ensure there are no undeclared charges or overbillings.

4. If you find an invalid charge, politely explain that you were not informed and will not pay it. If the hotel agrees to remove the charge, get written confirmation that it was done. Should the hotel refuse to remove the charge:

    - Ask to speak to the manager, and restate your case.
    - Say you will call your credit card company and block the charge as an unauthorized transaction. Then do it.
    - Vent your frustration on either the hotel's Facebook page, tripadvisor.com, or expedia.com.

DO THIS

ALWAYS ask for a discount when paying cash or staying multiple nights.

Out Negotiate the Priceline Negotiator

My heart pounded as if I had just played a big hand in Vegas.

I feared that I might actually get what I asked for. Using Priceline's Name Your Own Price feature, I bid a dirt cheap rate of $28 for a night's stay at a 3.5-star hotel. Flashes of dodgy motels, furniture with cigarette burns, and stained sheets filled my mind.

The way it works is you search for a hotel, just as you would at any other website, then Priceline asks you to "bid" how much you are willing to pay and requires that you provide your credit card information before submitting your bid. If your bid is accepted, Priceline automatically charges your credit card and sends you your reservation. Only then do you learn the exact hotel you will be staying at.

If you're wondering why anyone would play this game of hotel roulette, Priceline's "Name Your Own Price" feature has preferred rates that can be upwards of 25% to 50% off the rack rate for rooms, flight seats, car rentals, cruises, and vacation packages that are likely to go unsold.

Behind the scenes, Priceline compares your bid to the preferred Priceline rates offered by suppliers and accepts your bid if a supplier has provided a Priceline rate equal to or below your bid price.

Priceline comes with a number of catches, but there are ways to get around them and beat Priceline at its own game:

Catch #1

Priceline conceals the travel supplier's Priceline rate, and every dollar you bid above the Priceline rate is split between Priceline and the travel supplier.

Rule #1: Never bid a higher price than you can get from another website. Unless you do your homework, you can easily overpay and unnecessarily tether yourself to Priceline's inflexible booking terms.

To protect yourself, set your *bid ceiling,* which is the highest bid you are willing to make. This number has to be lower than the best fare you can get for an identical booking on any of the following websites: booking.com, tingo.com, kayak.com, travelpony.com.

Rule #2: Don't waste precious time unnecessarily rebidding.

To save yourself agony, set a bid floor that is within striking distance of the Priceline rate, and set your starting bid slightly below it. To do this:

- Priceline.com has a search engine that shows you winning Priceline bids on hotels in the last 30 days.

- biddingfortravel.com and hoteldealsrevealed.com have chat forums where Priceline users post their bid results. Simply look up the location you will be visiting to see what people have to say about their bid history.

- biddingtravelers.com is a website where Priceline bidders post their acceptance and rejection history. Before a recent trip to New York, I searched four-star hotels in Times Square and found that Priceline had recently:

    - Accepted three bids ranging from $135 to $250 per night.

    - Rejected three bids ranging from $140 to $157 per night.

I also learned that Priceline had issued a $150 counter offer on a $140 bid but also rejected a bid for that same amount on a similar date. The likely reason is that the bid that received the $150 counter offer was for four consecutive nights, whereas the $150 bid that was rejected was only for two nights.

Had you received the $150 counter offer and known this, you could reject the counter offer and submit another bid at $145/night with a good shot at saving another $5.

Catch #2

When Priceline rejects a bid, bidders have to wait 24 hours before they can rebid using identical criteria (date, hotel category, and area). When Priceline rejects a $100 bid for a four-star hotel in Times Square, it does not want you to continuously rebid in five dollar increments because that would make it easy for you to get the lowest available Priceline rate.

Work Around: If Priceline makes it too difficult to rebid, they will sabotage their business. Here are three ways you can thread the needle and rebid, without having to wait 24 hours:

i. Change all of the following three things in your rebid:

Credit card number

E-mail address

IP address

Having learned about credit card sign-up bonuses in chapter 4, you should have multiple credit cards. Multiple e-mail addresses are easy to get. To get around the IP address, you can delete your internet cookies, login from a different network, or bid from a different device.

ii. Have a travel buddy, friend, or family member rebid for you at a $5 increment.

iii. Change one of the following variables, so long as it does not compromise what you want:

Hotel Category: If you were rejected for a four-star hotel, rebid for a three-and-a-half star hotel.

Dates: If you can go anytime, submit rebids on alternate weekends.

Expand Your Area: Since Priceline cannot divulge hotel names until a bid is accepted, hotels are tagged to "areas" that you bid on. On the following page, you see that New York City is split into 19 areas and, to the left, you can select which areas to bid on:

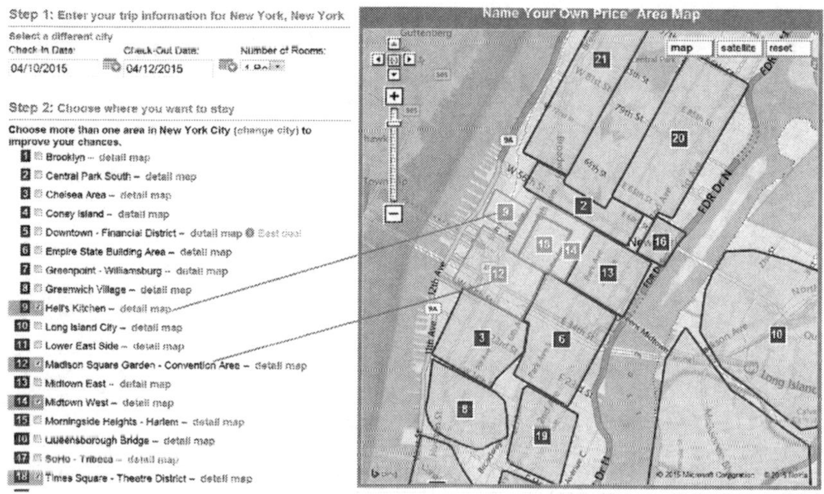

Scenarios:

Let's assume you can stay anywhere in the city: Start your search in your preferred area. If Priceline rejects your bid, gradually expand your search to include the next most desirable area and rebid.

If you need to be in a specific area on a set date:

Click on each of New York's areas one at a time to see which ones do not have any hotels in the category you want. Let's say you want to stay in a five-star hotel in Times Square, and Priceline rejected your bid. By looking at the picture on the next page, you can see that Morningside Heights does not have any five-star hotels because the '5-Star Luxury' line is greyed out. This means you can expand your search to also include area Morningside Heights and rebid at a $5 increment. If your second bid is rejected, you can submit a third bid at another $5 increment by expanding your search to include Queensborough Bridge without having to worry about being assigned to a hotel there. That's because Queensborough Bridge does not have any 5-star hotels either.

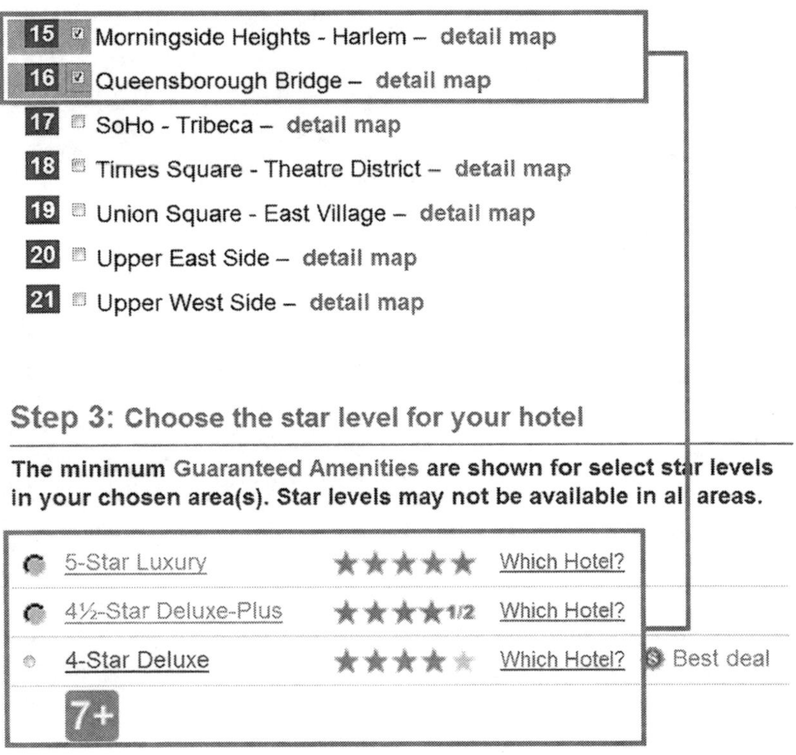

Catch #3

Upon accepting a bid, Priceline automatically charges your credit card, in accordance with its no-refund, no-change, no-cancellation policy.

Work Around: When keying your billing information, use a Visa or MasterCard gift card that has a lower balance than your bid amount. If Priceline accepts your bid, the gift card will have insufficient funds, and you will get a pop-up window saying, "We're sorry, the amount of this transaction exceeds the available balance …"

The moment you see this, you know that Priceline has accepted your bid, and you can submit a lower bid.

Catch #4

All purchases are final – No Changes, No Cancellations, No Refunds

Work Around: Pay for your booking with a credit card that offers trip-cancellation insurance. Eligible reasons for reimbursement vary slightly by policy, they generally include a doctor's note saying you are sick and unable to travel on your travel dates, a police report saying you could not get to the airport because of a traffic incident, job loss, jury duty, and death or grave illness in your immediate family.

If you don't have a credit card that offers trip-cancellation insurance, Priceline offers an option to purchase travel insurance before you submit your bid, and the policy terms are similar to those you get with many credit card benefits.

Great Hotel Websites

For the Nighthawk

bookadayroom.com offers discounts for daytime-only stays.

Last Minute Accommodations

hoteltonight.com offers heavily discounted hotel rooms for same day stays.

lastminute.com is where hotels try to sell off blocks of empty rooms that are likely to go unsold in the next few days.

room77.com shows you the view by room number. Hotel staff post their feedback on rooms, along with explanations about how their hotels operate.

For the Distinguished Traveler

wantmegetme.com: Find free upgrades, special treatment, and Wi-Fi at five-star hotels.

For Last Minute Travel Packages

lastminute.com

lastminutetravel.com

travelocity.com

travelzoo.com

tripadvisor.com

More Great Websites

backbid.com: Post your booking for competing hotels to see so they can send you counteroffers.

eurocheapo.com showcases cheap hotels in Europe.

hotels.com offers one free night for every 10 bookings.

trivago.com scours 650,000 hotel listings, from more than 150 websites.

For a comprehensive list of travel websites, the BEST PRICE section of breakthetravelbarrier.com neatly organizes websites for accommodations from least to most expensive.

9
Transportation
Travel Further for Less

Once you hit the road, you can redirect your day-to-day funds for gas, transit, and parking, to cover your basic public transit, shuttle buses, and taxi fares while traveling. By keeping these costs within your home transportation budget, these incidentals are not actually costing you anything more than if you were at home. As for big ticket transportation costs, let's start with a glimpse into the future of air travel ...

"No Frills Airline (NFA) offers subway straps to its passengers. The first one is free, if two are required, that will cost five dollars. Of course, seats are offered at $10. Seat belts are an additional five bucks. Overhead bins may be used for a five dollar fee per bag. Under seat stowage is only two dollars.

If a passenger needs to talk to a flight attendant, that will cost five dollars. Lavatory usage is a bargain: only 50 cents. There is a landing fee of $10 per passenger. Since the crew is supplied with parachutes, if insufficient funds are collected, the crew may, at its option, bail out. Any passenger who is a qualified pilot may land the plane, if they use a credit card to gain access to the flight deck. The fee for this is $500.

The airline's motto is "We Make Safe Trips Most of the Time." So, take a chance. What the heck.

The Dallas-Fort Worth airport is now charging two dollars to use electrical outlets while you wait for your flight. Want to use your notebook computer or charge your mobile phone? Pony up. The airport could install bars across the seats. Put in a buck and the bar retracts. There is a fee per bag to check luggage. But wait! The Skycaps do not get the fee, the airlines do. So, now the Skycap wants a tip in addition. Why stop there? How about a fee for reading the monitors? Want to check your flight? Put in a buck. Next will be a fee for using moving sidewalks, and a fee for using the tram between terminals. Since everyone has to go through security, why not charge for expedited service—the snob line. Then, the airline could charge for expedited boarding. Pay a fee, and get on ahead of the rabble. [5]"

Inside the Mind of an Airline Executive

Airlines have two goals:

1. Increase revenue without touching the posted rate.

The posted rate is an influential factor in deciding whether to fly so airlines protect this number and keep it low, by posting bare bones, no-frills rates and making up the difference through surcharges and discretionary fees. Unfortunately, this trend is getting to an extreme, and it is likely to continue to devolve until government intervenes with regulations that impose minimum standards and improved price transparency on everything from minimum seat size to limits for discretionary surcharges.

Airlines also know that the further out you book, the more likely it is that you will have to make a change. So they entice you to book your flight months out at discounted rates, knowing they will more than recoup the discount with hefty change fees.

2. Get paid now for services not rendered.

The further out you book your flight, the happier the airline is because you are paying them for a service they have not rendered and may never need to. Airlines overbook flights on the bet there will be enough people who do not appear or who change their itinerary that they will be able to pocket the overbooked revenue. It's like selling more tickets to a sporting event than there are seats.

Airlines fear having empty seats on planes, and every empty seat is a gamble gone wrong by the airline, which monitors progressive seat sales months before a plane takes off. Fares drop when bookings fall behind and they increase as the number of empty seats drop. The most profitable seats on a flight are those that are sold at a premium, at the last minute, to inflexible fliers who suddenly need to be on that flight.

Save Money on Every Flight – For the Rest of Your Life

Even though you know how to stockpile rewards points for free flights, it's unlikely you will amass enough points to cover every flight you take for the rest of your life. That's when the rest of this chapter comes in handy:

I. Should I pay or redeem my points?

II. Get two flights for the price of one (plus change fees).

III. Find the best price in 15 minutes flat, using the Fast Tracker on page 142.

IV. Shred airline costs and dodge fees.

I. Should I Pay or Redeem Points?

Just because you have enough points to redeem for a free flight does not mean you should automatically use them. Just as you would choose a $380 fare over a $427 fare for the same service, you need to treat your rewards points like cash. By comparing the relative value of your points to cash, you can use the one that offers the best value.

What's a Point Worth?

At the time this was written:

- Long-haul, round trip domestic flights can be redeemed for 25,000 points.
- A standard industry benchmark representing the average cost of a round trip domestic flight in the U.S. is $352, before tax.

If you divide the average cost of a domestic flight ($352) by the number of points needed for that same flight (25,000), you get 0.014, which tells you that, on average, a point is worth 1.4 cents. This means you should:

- Pay cash if your points cannot earn you at least 1.4 cents per point.
- Redeem points anytime they are costing you less than 1.4 cents to redeem.

Let's say you have a number of trips coming up, and you want to pay for these flights using the means that give you the best value:

i. For each flight, determine how many points you must redeem.

ii. Use the Fast Tracker on page 142 to find the best fare.

iii. Divide:

a. The before-tax cost of the flight

by

b. The number of redeemable points for that same flight

The higher your result is, the more value you are getting for your points. For example, if you have 100,000 points and you plan to visit Rio, Mumbai, and Florence this year:

Destination	Cost	Points	Point Value	Pay / use points?
Rio	$1,250	40,000	$1,200/40,000 = 0.03	Redeem points
Mumbai	$2,400	90,000	$2,200/90,000 = 0.0244	Pay
Florence	$1,600	60,000	$1,600/60,000 = 0.0266	Redeem points

In this case, the Mumbai flight is the most expensive of the three flights, but you should pay for it anyway because the Rio and Florence flights offer better value for your points. Had you redeemed 90,000 points for the Mumbai flight, you would only have 10,000 points left over, which are not enough to use for either of the remaining flights. Combined, those flights cost $450 more than the Mumbai flight.

In the above example, we did not factor in points you would have earned from paying for your flight and applied toward a future flight. Let's say you would earn 750 points by paying for a flight, calculate the net value of those points and factor them into your decision as follows:

i. Multiply 750 by the industry standard target point value, which is 0.014 (or 1.4 cents) to get $10.50.

ii. Subtract $10.50 from the price of your plane ticket. In the case of the Mumbai flight, it would leave you with $2,389.50.

You have now factored in the value of the points you are earning for paying for your Mumbai flight and can now do the same for Rio and Florence.

If you ever find yourself in the envious position of having enough points to cover every flight you plan to take in the next year, save yourself the hassle of doing the math, and just use your points. After all, that's what they're for.

II. Turn a Flight into a Halfway-Around-the-World Ticket

Let's say you are planning a trip to Budapest and would like to visit London, Paris, or Amsterdam along the way. Instead of booking separate flights to each destination, look for a flight to Budapest that connects through either of these cities. If you can find a route with a departing connection in one of those cities (for example, London) and a return flight with a connection in another (for example, Amsterdam), even better. Instead of booking your flight online, call the airline and ask them to book your flight but to book the first leg of your flight a few days earlier than the second leg. The airline will charge you a service fee, which will likely be much less expensive than booking your flight online and then paying change fees to extend your connections into stopovers.

If you decide to extend a connection and your flight is already booked, you will need to review your airline's terms, conditions, and rates for change fees and stopovers.

Keep in mind:

- Change fees vary by carrier and class of ticket; although they can be free under certain circumstances, change fees average between $50 and $200.
- Third-party websites often come with no-change policies and high change fees.
- If the leg you are rerouting to is more expensive than your original route, you will have to pay the difference.

Free Flight Secret #39

Next time you book a one-way flight home, decide on a place you would later like to visit that:

a. Connects through your home city from your point of origin,

AND

b. Costs the same (or less) as flying directly home (it applies equally, whether paying with cash or redeeming points).

Now, book a flight from your current location to your next vacation destination that connects through your home city. Then, call the airline and ask to have your connection in your home city extended into a stopover, until the date you want to take your next trip. Airlines require that all legs of a trip be complete within a certain timeframe from the departure date. Check to see what the allowable lag time is to complete all legs of your flight. A long as you stay within it ... PRESTO!

By extending connections into stopovers, you can visit two to three times as many destinations for the cost of change fees. And, if you do this while flying on rewards points, you can fly on next to nothing.

Fast Tracker

Find the Best Price in 15 Minutes Flat, without Any Games or Guesswork

Before You Start – There are two things you need to know:

1. Some travel websites have been found to display higher fares in the following circumstances:

- Mac computers sometimes show higher prices than identical searches run at the same time on Windows. The theory behind this price differential is that some websites believe Mac owners tend to spend more than Windows owners; therefore, the websites raise prices for searches run on Mac computers.

- If cookies are enabled on your PC, your search history stays on file, and websites can detect your search history. This can reveal your purchasing habits and intentions so don't be surprised if the price has increased, when you return to your PC to book your flight.

2. There is no single website that will get you the best price every time. That said, there are a few websites that return better fares, more often, on average than others. They are:

hipmunk.com

kayak.com

skyscanner.com

These websites often return fares within a few dollars of each other. But, sometimes, fares vary quite bit, with no consistent pattern. That's why you need to use all three.

Scenario 1

"I know exactly where I'm going."

"I can go anytime."

To find a rock bottom rate, run your search through these three websites and cherry-pick the flight that is best for you:

hipmunk.com

kayak.com

skyscanner.com

"What if my results are all too expensive?"

If You're Willing to Hold off for a Better Price:

Open an account with one of the following websites. Then enter the information of the best flight fare you found to receive email notifications anytime lower fares occur:

farecompare.com

yapta.com

If You Aren't Patient:

i. Toggle between one-way and round trip flights, as one-way fares are sometimes less than half the cost of a round trip flight. Just keep in mind that whatever money you save on the one-way fare, you may need to cough up to get home.

ii. Consider flying each way on different airlines. Kayak's search engine is multi-airline friendly and will mix and match airlines, to better accommodate your search parameters.

iii. Expand your search to include:

- All area airports: Cities like London, New York, and Vancouver each have six airports.
- Neighboring cities: In the case of the $1,276 L.A.-to-Paris fare, expand your search to surrounding cities for better fares. Domestic flights in the U.S. and continental Europe are often very cheap so you can take the last leg of your trip inexpensively and come out ahead. Just factor in the risk of delays to give yourself enough time between legs.

Now … Make That Great Online Fare Ultra-Economical

Find "Hidden" Fares: Call the airline with the best fare and ask whether it can find a better fare than the one you found online. I did this after finding a $715 return flight to London, and the agent told me there was an even cheaper rate of $689. When I asked why I couldn't see it online, the agent responded that I could, if I searched at the right times, but couldn't tell me exactly when those times were. Crazy, but true. If your agent finds you a cheaper fare, ask for a screenshot or formal airline itinerary will all the flight details, including the fare, and read this entire section before you do anything.

Currency Advantage: You can save big dollars using websites based in lower currency countries. Flightnetwork.com allows you to book flights on just about any airline, anywhere in the world. Since all fares are charged in Canadian dollars, and the Canadian dollar is trading well below the U.S. dollar at the time of this writing, Americans are saving 15% to 20% on the currency differential alone, by booking domestic flights on Flight Network. Europeans using Flight Network are saving 26% on the currency exchange alone, and British travelers are saving a whopping 46%. If you do this, book your flight with a credit card that waives foreign transaction fees such as the ones below:

- U.S. Cards: Discover It, Capital One and Capital One Quicksilver, AMEX Platinum
- Canadian Cards: Marriott Rewards Visa, Amazon.ca

Best Price Guarantees are policies where travel suppliers agree to match lower fares offered through other websites for an identical flight. Some travel suppliers even offer an additional credit you can apply toward a future flight such as the following promotions in place at the time of this writing:

- Air France matches lower fares offered on their flights via other websites.
- Priceline refunds double the difference between Priceline's fare and the lower fare.
- Fare match + $100 Credit: Alaska Air, Delta, JetBlue, United
- Fare match + $50 Credit: American, Air Canada, Expedia, Orbitz
- Fare match + $10 Credit: Flight Network (Applies to fares offered by Canadian travel agencies, including expedia.ca)

To see the latest best price guarantee promotions, visit "BEST PRICE" at breakthetravelbarrier.com.

Many fliers make the mistake of booking their flight before looking for lower fares. Best price guarantees generally only allow fliers to submit claims in the 24 hours after booking their flight. Instead, look for flights that qualify for a best price guarantee before you book. To do this:

1. Look up the fares offered by travel suppliers that offer $50 and $100 credits on top of their best price guarantee.
2. Then try to find a lower fare for an identical itinerary on kayak, skyscanner, and hipmunk. If you find a cheaper identical fare:

    i. Take a screenshot of the cheaper fare.

    ii. Book the more expensive option.

    iii. Submit your lower price claim right away to get refunded the difference AND the credit.

Price Drop Refund Policies: If you book your flight with an airline that offers a price drop refund policy, you can book your flight now and also be refunded the difference between what you pay and any subsequent price drops. For example, at the time this was written, Alaska Airlines and Flightnetwork.com were offering refunds for subsequent price drops of any amount. Additionally, the following airlines were offering refunds for price drops exceeding the following amounts:

Over $25: Westjet

Over $75: Jetblue Airways, AirTran Airways, Virgin America

Over $100: Hawaiian Airlines

Over $200: American Airlines, Delta, United, US Airways

To see the latest price drop refund policies, visit "BEST PRICE" at breakthetravelbarrier.com.

These policies often come with a number of restricting terms and conditions. Here are some of the common ones along with a few strategies for getting around them:

1. **Limit One Claim Per Booking:** If you claim a $5 price drop, you'll miss out if the price keeps plunging. On the flip side, you'll leave money on the table if you hold off in hopes of a 25% price drop. Treat price drop policies like insurance; you aren't concerned about a small price drop, but you want to get something back if it drops hard. Set yourself a 10% to 15% floor, and claim your refund as soon as it falls below it. I set my floor at 10% and I'm happy any time I get it, regardless of how much further the price drops.

2. **Fliers Must Submit a Claim for Refund:** Most operators don't provide refunds you unless you submit a claim (tingo.com is an exception but this site is exclusively for hotels). Alaska Airlines and Flight Network do not offer price drop email notifications, so set up an account with one of these websites with your flight details. You'll get real-time price drop e-notifications to check your airline's website for price drops.

   farecompare.com

   yapta.com

3. **Heavy Change and Cancellation Penalties**: To get around no cancellation/transfer policies and hefty change fees, pay with a credit card that offers trip cancellation insurance that entitles you to a refund if you have to cancel at a later date. Qualifying reasons vary slightly by policy but generally include:

   i. A doctor's note saying you are sick and unable to travel on your flight date. If you are unable to travel due to illness while abroad, you can claim the cost of your doctor's visit through your global travel insurance.

   ii. A police report saying you could not get to the airport due to a traffic incident.

   iii. Death or grave illness in your immediate family.

   iv. Loss of employment.

If you cannot travel for any of these reasons, cancel your flight and submit the bill and required documentation to the insurance provider to collect your refund.

Keep in mind, travel supplier terms and conditions may also:

- Cap the maximum refund amount. For example, Flight Network limits the refund amount for international flights to $200.
- Have blackout periods shortly before departure. For example, Flight Network disallows claims for vacation packages in the 31 prior to departure.
- Restrict price drop claims to:
    - Economy class tickets
    - The first 72 hours after booking a flight

Scenario 2

"I know exactly where I'm going."

"Dates are firm, I'm not flexible."

Go to hipmunk.com or matrix.itasoftware.com for a calendar showing you each day's best fare on your desired route. If your search results are all too expensive, go to page 144 and follow the steps under "What if my results are all too expensive?"

Scenario 3

"I'll go anywhere, get me the best deal out of town."

"I'm limited to a specific time window."

To find the cheapest flight departing from your home airport every day, for a given timeframe, go to skyscanner.com and:

- Select a one-way flight from your departure airport.
- Leave the destination field blank.
- Select the time period for which you want to see the cheapest flights. It can be a day, week, month, or year.

You can also find the cheapest flights by location at kayak.com, under the "Explore" option.

If your search results are all too expensive, go to page 144 and follow the steps under *"What if my results are all too expensive?"*

Scenario 4

"I need an inexpensive place to sleep now.
No games, no guesswork."

When you need to find a place right away, start at the top of the following list, which sorts accommodation options from least to most expensive. By sticking to this order, the first option you find is apt to also be your least expensive option:

1. Free Accommodations:

- Friends and family
- Sleep in your car
- Redeem hotel rewards/loyalty points

2. Paid Accommodations:

i. Camping – National Campground Directories: campingcheque.com: Access more than 640 campsites in 29 countries for 16 Euros a night.

Australia: camping.com.au

Canada: camping-canada.com

Europe: campingeurope.com, eurocampings.co.uk, europe-camping-holiday.com, camping.info

New Zealand: tourism.net.nz:

U.S. & Canada: uscampgrounds.info

ii. Hostels – Best International Hostel Websites:

hostelbookers.com: Offers a lowest price guarantee and does not charge booking fees.

hostelworld.com: You can browse user reviews, and the app has GPS integration to find places nearby.

iii. Last Minute Hotels:

bookadayroom.com: For discounted day time stays.

hoteltonight.com: Select your city, and get a list of heavily discounted rooms for that night.

lastminute.com: Lists hotels offloading blocks of empty rooms likely to go unsold.

room77.com: Shows you the view by room number. Hotel staff post their feedback on rooms, along with explanations about how their hotels operate.

Scenario 5

"The airport is a 45 minute drive to my final destination."

Taxis are extremely expensive and rides can run you more than $100 in cities where airports are far from your final destination.

Alternatives to Taxis:

- **Public transit** (subway, city buses) is your most economical option for inner city transportation. It can sometimes be more convenient than alternate options.
- **Airport train:** A quick Google search before a trip to London could save you a 100 Euro taxi ride, as you would learn that the Heathrow Express departs Heathrow toward downtown every 15 minutes for just 20 Euros.

- **Split a taxi with others:** If you happen to meet people during your flight who are heading to the same area, propose sharing a cab and splitting the cost.

- **Shuttle buses:**
  - o If you're staying at a hotel or resort, ask if they offer shuttle service to/from the airport.
  - o Some cities have airport shuttles that service the downtown core. You can find information about airport shuttles on each airport's website.

- **When taxiing alone:**
  - o Before you get in: Make sure you know the going rate from the airport to your destination.
  - o Before your cab moves: Mention the going rate for this route and say a few things that suggest you've been there before. This way, your cabbie won't take the scenic route. If you don't do this and your meter runs to $150, you won't have a leg to stand on.

- **Car Rentals:** Unless you are visiting a densely populated city or a hotel with expensive parking charges, car rentals can be less expensive than taking taxis and provide much greater freedom. For more information on how to get the best price for a car rental, go to page 163.

Scenario 6

"I'm flying halfway around the world, and wish I could see other destinations on route. The problem is I can't afford to book any more flights."

The Solution:

I use this trick all the time, including three times in the last four months for stopovers in Chicago, Phoenix, and Tokyo:

1. Use the following websites to find flights to your destination that have connections in cities you would also like to visit. If you find a flight that connects through multiple cities, even better!

    matrix.itasoftware.com

    hipmunk.com

    skyscanner.com

2. Once you find a route that interests you, call the airline, and ask them to book your flight. But ask them to book the first leg of your flight a few days earlier than the second leg, as outlined in how to "Turn a Flight into a Halfway-Around-the-World Ticket" on page 140. The airline will charge a service fee, which will likely be much less expensive than booking your flight online and then paying change fees to extend your connections into stopovers.

If your flight is already booked, find out what the airline charges for change fees, and what their policies are for extending connections into stopovers. If you are booking through a third-party website, you also need to obtain the same terms and conditions from the third-party operator. Assuming you are fine with the airline's change fee and stopover policies, book your flight.

A True Story of Lavish Excess

If you had the option of using your $400,000 mortgage to get unlimited flights, for yourself and a guest for the rest of your life, would you use it for the flights or for a home? Just imagine the possibilities:

- You could fly to your favorite sporting event every weekend.
- You could take the red eye to the Cannes film festival, watch movies all day, then fly home that night.

Until 2002, American Airlines sold unlimited lifetime flight passes for $200,000, and a companion pass could be added for an additional $150,000. When American Airlines realized that some holders of these lifetime passes were practically living on their planes, they shelved the passes, which were costing them millions more than they were making. If you ever hear of a lifetime pass sale again, please write to me right away, and I promise to use my new lifetime pass to fly to your hometown and thank you personally.

Shred Airline Costs and Dodge Fees

Checked Bag Fees

There are three ways your luggage can cost you money: packing too heavy, bags that are too big, and bringing too many bags.

Here are five ways you can get around checked bag fees:

1. Pay for your flight using a credit card that offers a free checked bag benefit. For the latest list of credit cards you can use, go to "NO MORE FEES" at breakthetravelbarrier.com.

2. Travel with a luggage jacket, available at jaktogo.com.

3. Prioritize airlines that do not charge to check bags. kayak.com posts checked bag allowances by airline.

4. Limit your luggage to comply with carry-on restrictions.

5. Earn elite airline status or fly first class, which often offers free checked bag benefits.

Booking Fees

Travel agents and customer service people generally do not charge you until they book your itinerary. It is standard, however, for travel agents to collect a non-refundable deposit—that you can later apply to your booking—in cases where they have to do time-intensive research, such as drafting an itinerary for an around the world trip.

To get around fees charged for bookings made over the telephone, politely explain that you want to book your itinerary online, but you will not have internet access for the foreseeable future. Since you generally do not get charged for booking directly through travel suppliers, there is a chance the agent may be sympathetic to your situation and waive your fee.

Before you book through a third-party website, check to see if they charge a booking fee. If so, go straight to the airline's website to avoid the booking fee, and check to see whether you can get the same price that was offered on the third-party website.

Round the World Tickets

Using just one plane ticket, you can get to just about any eight short list destinations you have, anywhere in the world, for the price many people pay to fly round trip between the U.S. and Australia. It's called a "round the world ticket," and there are two ways you can build your custom trip.

1. Travel agents can refer you to an agent who specializes in them. All an agent needs is a list of the places you want to visit and the places you need to be on specific dates. From there, the agent does all the research and drafts a custom itinerary for you.
2. There are a number of websites that offer resources you can use to build your own round the world itinerary including:
    a. airtreks.com is a leader in providing affordable, custom, efficient international air tickets for complex multi-stop international journeys.
    b. Major Airline Alliances have a page dedicated to round the world itineraries. They are:
        - oneworld.com
        - skyteam.com
        - staralliance.com

When planning an around the world trip, devote each leg to long-haul flights. If you want to visit nearby destinations, use budget regional carriers and ground transportation to get around, once you're there.

Keep in mind, the cheapest round the world tickets are non-refundable and come with no change and no cancellation policies. If you go with an inexpensive ticket that comes with these restrictive terms, you should, at the very least, pay for your ticket with a credit card that offers trip cancellation insurance, for the reasons we covered on page 148.

Overbooked Flights

Every once in a while, you will be boarding a flight and will hear the agent asking for volunteers willing to stay behind, due to an over-booked flight. If you're flexible, ask the agent what they will offer as compensation for waiting for a later flight. You will usually be offered a cash voucher for a future flight and a food coupon to use while you wait. If there are no other volunteers, give the impression that what they have to offer doesn't interest you, and the agent may up the ante.

Summary

Where to Look

- If you only use one travel website, you are paying more than you need to.
- Regional airlines are generally cheaper than national carriers.
- For international flights, search airlines from both countries and take the currency difference into account, to determine which one is cheaper.
- The Fast Tracker, starting on page 142, shows you how to find the best price in 15 minutes flat, by travel scenario.

When to Book

If you aren't flexible, book three to six months out for cheaper flights.

When to Fly

- Peak times (holidays, weekends, peak business travel times) are the most expensive.
- The earliest flights of the day are usually cheapest, especially indirect flights.
- There is endless speculation about which days are more or less expensive than others. Price is ultimately driven by supply and demand so prices will be cheaper where demand is low.

Last Minute Travel

- Flying standby isn't what it used to be.
- If you aren't flexible, don't count on getting a last minute deal.
- If you are flexible, the best last minute deals are often all-inclusive vacation packages for cruises and resorts.

Minimize Surcharges

- Always understand the terms and conditions before you pay.
- If your airline charges for paper boarding passes, take the electronic version and download it to your device.
- Avoid connecting through airports that charge high airport taxes. For example, flights connecting through Frankfurt pay less tax than those flying through Heathrow in London.

Ground Transportation

Just as accommodations were organized from least-to-most expensive options, you now have ground transportation options laid out the same way. Start at the top of the list, and work your way down. The first option you come across that suits your needs is likely also your most economical option.

I. Hitchhiking

II. Bicycle

III. Public Transit

IV. Shuttle Buses

V. Rail and Bus

VI. Road Trip by Car

VII. Car Rentals

VIII. Taxis

I. Hitchhiking

Although many people have hitchhiked and had good experiences doing so, I personally do not advocate hitchhiking because you run the risk of finding yourself unable to get out of a situation of your own free will. It is not my intention to alarm you, I just want to empower you to travel economically while always being in control.

II. Bicycle

Some places are easier to see by bike and allow you to cover much more ground than by foot. This is how I saw the area from the Fisherman's Wharf and the Golden Gate Bridge in San Francisco. In cities like Amsterdam, it would be a crime not to take a bike ride along the canal.

Public transit systems are increasingly offering public bicycles, which are both convenient and economical. Before you visit a destination, look up their public transit information online to see if they offer bicycle rentals.

A friend of mine rents bikes from local bicycle shops that do not normally rent bikes. She always gets better prices than through rental companies, and they are always glad to help.

III. Public Transit

Not only is public transit economical, it's also the best way to explore large cities. Prior to leaving on a trip, do a quick Google search to see whether public transit connects directly to the airport. If you plan on using public transit during your stay, look for passes that offer unlimited rides per day, week, or month. Some transit systems also offer discounts for bulk discounts like:

- Parts of the U.K. allow four people to ride for the price of two.
- The Munich U-Bahn airport has bulk rate for purchases of eight or more passes.

IV. Road Trip by Car

You (or your grandparents) may remember the 1950s commercial "See the USA in your Chevrolet." If you're going on a long road trip, get an oil change before you leave and, if you have an older car, the cost of having a basic inspection done is worth the money, especially if it averts being stranded on the side of the freeway.

Triple A (AAA)

AAA acts as an extension to your car insurance for costs related to roadside assistance. Whether your car breaks down, runs out of gas, or you lock yourself out, you won't have to pay out-of-pocket for help. I have heard of cases where car passengers were able to use their AAA cards, when stranded with drivers who are not AAA members.

The cost of a AAA membership varies by package but generally ranges between $50 and $150 a year. Keep your card in your wallet, and file a copy of it in the cloud, in case you ever need it and do not have the actual card with you.

Valet Services

Some valet car companies charge daily rates, while others charge per drop off. If the charge is per drop off, you might want to skip the valet, especially if you plan on coming and going all day.

V. Shuttle Buses

If you cannot connect to public transit from your airport, there are likely shuttle buses that run a circuit between the airport, downtown, and touristy areas. A number of hotels also offer shuttle services, not only to and from the airport but also to local events and popular destinations.

VI. Rail and Bus

All roads lead to seat61.com which is the most comprehensive website devoted to ground travel worldwide. It has everything you need to find rail transportation, and you can buy your rail pass directly on their website.

"Will Sing for Travel"

If you can sing, tell jokes, pull magic tricks, or educate passengers, Canadian rail company Via Rail might offer you a free ride for entertaining passengers on route. Showcase your talent at viarail.ca under "How to Contact Us" and you might score yourself a free trip along the same route Joshua Jackson followed in the movie "One Week."

VII. Car Rentals

Some places are just best experienced by car. Whether you will be driving along the Mediterranean coast or through Yellowstone National Park, when you book your car rental at autoslash.com, the website continuously crawls the internet for lower fares and, if it finds one, will automatically cancel your original reservation and rebook you at the lower fare.

Be Careful

Some countries charge a premium for automatic transmission. If you aren't sure whether this is the case for your rental, make sure you ask or rent a manual (stick shift) transmission.

Cardinal Rules for Car Rentals

1. Always book economy, even if you want a midsize or premium vehicle. It isn't uncommon for the rental company to run out of economy cars and, when this happens, they automatically upgrade you.

- If this works and you get a free upgrade: Ask for an additional discount, to compensate for the added cost of fuel for the bigger vehicle.

- If you don't get the upgrade you were hoping for: Wait to see what car is assigned to you. If you aren't crazy about it, ask about an upgrade at that time. Last minute upgrades can be inexpensive, especially if there is a surplus of cars in the lot, in which case every dollar the rental company gets from an upgrade is earned at no extra cost to them.

2. Instead of paying for collision insurance, ask your auto insurance company whether your auto insurance extends to cover collision on car rentals. If not, book your car rental using a credit card that has collision insurance benefits.

VIII. Taxis

Milan, Italy, October 9, 2011.

"There's no rush, let's finish our glass of wine." Ten minutes passed from the moment I said that until we descended to our taxi, where the meter was already at 25 Euros and counting! Our driver either didn't speak English or played on the excuse that he couldn't and, as I complained, the meter kept rising; and we had yet to move a foot!

This was not the only time that the taxis got me on this trip. Two weeks earlier, I stumbled of out my Munich hotel room hours after Oktoberfest's closing ceremony to head for the airport, only to find the subway was closed. The 60 Euros I saved for booking my 6 a.m. flight evaporated, when I found myself having to pay $85 Euros to take a cab from downtown Munich to the airport.

All this is to say that taxis are extremely expensive, and you want to avoid them as much as possible. Make the most of public transit, shuttle buses, and the daily rate for a car rental, which is often less than a single taxi ride.

If you find yourself having to take a taxi:

- If you meet people on your flight who are going to the same area, invite them to share a cab with you and split the cost.
- Do your homework. Know the going rate for your route, and negotiate your price before you get in.
- To save yourself from getting taken for a scenic ride, do a little homework so you can say a few things to your driver that suggest you know the area.
- In cities like Las Vegas, you can rent a stretch limousine for $80 to $100 an hour, which is cheaper than taxi rides that last just as long.

10

Fund Your Travels

Cost cutting is only half of the battle. You can cut your costs to zero, but life costs money and, unless you also have money coming in, you will not be able to make ends meet. Here are five ways you can fund your travels and further offset your travel costs.

1. Work While Traveling

Athens, Greece, June 2014:

Dan is a skipper who spends his summers chartering small groups along the Adriatic Coast. As he stocks his yacht, Dan's clients board and greet him like an old friend. Not only does Dan have a dream summer job, he also gets paid to attend travel shows in the off-season, selling yacht holidays. That's where the passengers met Dan; he personally sold them the trip. You might not get Dan's dream job, but, fortunately, there are many ways to find work while traveling.

Most western and Commonwealth countries have work visa programs that make it easy for students and young professionals under the age of 30 to get a temporary international work permit. To start, goabroad.com and gooverseas.com offer resources about international work programs, internships, volunteer, and study opportunities. In addition, transitionsabroad.com helps young Americans find accommodations, meaningful work, and study terms abroad.

International Employment Agencies

- ccusa.com: Helps travelers find teaching positions, camp counseling jobs, and volunteer placements in over 50 countries.
- theworkingholidayclub.com: Helps travelers from Australia, New Zealand, and Britain find work in the U.K., U.S., Canada, Australia, and New Zealand.
- workpermit.com: Offers information on how to obtain work permits by country.

Find a Job That Is Right for You

In addition to the traditional travel friendly jobs you find in restaurants, hotels, and resorts, here are some unconventional jobs that may interest you:

- americanhiking.org: Repair hiking trails for pay or room and board.
- care.com: Find housekeeping, nanny, and pet sitting opportunities.
- Work as a group travel guide with a group travel operator, such as such as G Adventures, Go-Today, Free & Easy Traveler, and Intrepid Travel. Travel Guides can often transfer to tours in other parts in the world at the end of their term.

- National parks and ski resorts often post international work opportunities directly on their website. For example, you can try yellowstonejobs.com and whistlerblackcomb.com.

- Campgrounds, RV parks, and hostels sometimes offer a free place to stay in exchange for work.

- Teaching English abroad can earn you more than a paycheck. There is no deeper way to immerse yourself than to teach local children, and it will leave you with the satisfaction of having made a difference in the lives of others. If you are considering teaching abroad, I recommend you get TESL certified. It's an internationally recognized certificate to teach English as a second language, it costs about $1,000, and it will put you ahead of others who do not have it.

    - languagecourse.net: Explains how to get TESOL and TESL certified.

    - gooverseas.com: Posts international English teaching jobs.

- Cruise ships – You can bypass much of the bureaucracy of needing to obtain a work visa by working on international waters. Allcruisejobs.com and cruiselinejobs.com offer information on how to get into the cruise line industry. To find a job, you can browse job postings at carnival.com, celebrity.com, hollandamerica.com, ncl.com, princess.com, and royalcaribbean.com. In addition, routesinternational.com has a directory of North American cruise lines you can also search for jobs.

- Airline employees have a benefit to cherish in the form of flights and buddy passes. I know a flight attendant who is strictly an emergency reserve on weekends so that she can hang on to her flight benefits.

TIP

If you work abroad, open a checking account with a local bank account so that you don't have to deal with currency exchange and transfer fees.

2. Take a Year off Work

The young and retired are free to spread their wings, teachers get their summers off, then there are the rest of us. That doesn't mean we can't take extended vacations, too:

> careerbreaksecrets.com: Offers tips and tricks for planning a career break.
>
> meetplango.com: Hosts events to help people planning their first career break.
>
> unitedplanet.org: Offers professionals opportunities to volunteer to causes abroad during their career breaks.
>
> gapyear.com: Is a British-based website that offers international internships.

A teacher I know found a creative way to keep getting paid during his year-long trek around the world. Four years prior to his trip, he made an arrangement with the school board to withhold 20% of his salary for four years. During those years, he received 80% of his salary. During his gap year, the school board continued paying him using the portion of his salary they had retained.

Ways to offset your at-home expenses when traveling long-term:

- Offer your place as a short-term rental, using the same websites you use to find accommodations while traveling.
- Freeze your gym membership.
- Suspend your cable and internet services.
- Turn off all electricity, heat, and air conditioning. If you live in a sub-zero climate, keep the temperature high enough to keep anything from freezing.
- If you will be away for a month or more, consider downgrading your auto insurance to basic comprehensive. This will lower your insurance payments, and your vehicle will still be protected against fire, theft, damage, and vandalism.

3. Travel for a Cause

If you will be traveling to contribute to a worthy cause, you will be amazed at how many people will be willing to open their wallets and support you. Whether you want to study abroad, take a dream honeymoon, or help underprivileged children in Africa, crowdfunding is a ground breaking new way you can fund your travels.

The reality is that most travel-based crowdfunding campaigns fail to raise more than a fraction of their goal. Although there have been cases of massively successful crowdfunding campaigns, they are usually restricted to cases where ill and underprivileged people need financial assistance to travel for medical or emergency purposes. So don't expect to fund your Caribbean cruise this way. But, if you are traveling for a worthy cause, you can run a successful crowdfunding campaign, if you do it right.

Let's say you are a competitive athlete or part of a group that wants to compete in an event abroad. You can run a successful online crowdfunding campaign by doing the following:

1. State your cause, with a personalized plea about your cause, why it's important, how it will make a difference, and how you will use the funds.

2. Offer something of value to those who donate.

3. Have a captivating title and include a video and pictures.

4. Show your appreciation to everyone that donates, be it a simple thank you or an act of kindness.

Let's say you have Africa on your radar of places to visit. You can fund your trip by contributing to a worthy cause there. A simple Google search of "Kenya daycare fundraising" returns all sorts of campaigns, including a climbing expedition put on by the Nasio Trust Center, which raises money for day care centers in Kenya. By signing up to the expedition, you can raise donations for the Nasio Trust Center through a crowdfunding campaign and also use a portion of those donations to offset your costs of traveling there for the expedition.

By using crowdfunding campaigns this way, you will likely have more success than 90% of all campaigns out there.

The most popular websites for travel crowdfunding campaigns include:

fundanything.com

fundly.com

fundrazr.com

gofundme.com

gogetfunding.com

peerbackers.com

For the latest list of travel friendly crowdfunding websites, visit "FUND YOUR TRAVELS" at breakthetravelbarrier.com. Before you decide which crowdfunding website to use, review the fee structures and terms of use. Although it's usually free to set up a profile, these websites generally retain about 5% of the funds raised, as their fee for the platform provided to you. If you run a successful campaign, 5% can add up to be a lot of money!

*For more information on the Nasio Trust Center, visit: thenasiotrust.org and go to "Get Involved." You will see that they also sponsor a 10K run in Britain, where 18 racers raised $5,000 Euros for a much needed vehicle for the day care centers.

4. Take Mini-Vacations while Attending Conferences

If you hold a professional designation or are part of a professional association that requires you to take ongoing continuing education courses to maintain your standing, you may be able to deduct a portion of your travel costs by attending conferences or workshops related to your profession, in cities you are planning to visit anyway, so long as the conference is not also offered significantly closer to your hometown. Allowable deductions vary, depending on where you live, so consult a tax professional to confirm which out-of-pocket expenses you can deduct. You can usually deduct at least one trip each year, including your transportation costs and a portion of your food and accommodation expenses, from the day prior to the start of the event until the day after it finishes.

By combining your continuing education with a vacation, you can often deduct a portion of your trip. To find conferences or workshops related to your profession, look up the local chapter websites of professional associations you belong to in cities you would like to visit. If you do not find any events at that time, sign up to their newsletter so that you get updates as conferences get scheduled.

5. Travel Writing – Profit from Your Passion

There is one secret most travel experts don't share about how they offset their own travel costs. It's how they fund their travels through their travel writing business. Don't discount this option as unrealistic. You don't need to be a columnist for Yahoo Travel nor do you need to be a full-time writer. There are no college degrees or professional designations to distinguish travel experts. You just need to be credible, have a message that resonates with others, and have a platform you can reach them on. Credibility comes from:

1. How many engaged followers you have.

2. The quality of your online presence, be it a blog, YouTube channel, published articles, or recorded interviews.

If you enjoy writing about and sharing your travel experiences, consider taking travel writing to the next level. It can be surprisingly easy to sell articles to community publications, local media, and school newspapers.

Although the pay through these mediums is insignificant (sometimes $50 or less), some compensation is better than nothing, and there perks, such as the Anthony Bourdain treatment. In return for providing publicity, you can get free tours and admission to events, complimentary dinners, and free accommodations. Just bear in mind that, as a travel writer, you have an ethical responsibility to write unbiased content so it's vital that you communicate to travel operators that your viewpoints will be based on your observations and experiences—good or bad—and that you cannot guarantee what spin your review will have.

Five Steps to Setting up a Writing Project

Before you start on your travel writing journey, you need at least one of the following:

i. An online platform through which you can reach an audience, be it a travel website, blog, and/or newsletter.

ii. A template you can use to pitch your articles to publications and media. At the back of this book, Appendix C is a Travel Writing Sales Template you can use to pitch your articles to publications.

Transform Wanderlust into a Sellable Message in Five Easy Steps:

1. **Find something to write about:** Think creatively about what would appeal to a mass audience.

2. **Find paying customers:** Look for local publications and websites that travelers are likely to read, and look up the contact information of their editors.

3. **Pitch your article:** Use the travel writing sales template in Appendix C at the back of this book to pitch editors.

4. **Follow up:** Two days after your pitch, follow up by phone. If the editor isn't interested, ask what would be of interest and adjust accordingly.

5. **Keep records** of all sales pitches and correspondence.

Deducting Expenses

Not only can you make money from travel writing, you may also be able to deduct certain costs directly related to writing projects.[6] Allowable deductions and limitations vary by jurisdiction so you need to consult a tax advisor. I use and recommend a tax advisor with expertise working with artistic entrepreneurs. That said, the most important factor in determining whether you can deduct travel writing expenses is whether you are a professional or leisurely travel writer. The distinction between the two can get fussy, but in general:

- Leisurely writers sell occasional articles and can generally deduct expenses up to the amount of revenue received for those articles.
- Professional travel writers generally rely on it as their primary source of income. They usually have a registered business and can deduct all expenses directly related to their writing.

The following types of expenses can generally be deducted, with the understanding that there are limits to how much you can deduct:

- Food, accommodation, and transportation (F.A.T.) while traveling.
- Excursion fees, admission costs, and expenses incurred to write the article.
- Out-of-pocket expenses that would not have been incurred had you not written the article (fitness centers, hotel movies, etc.).

If you write from home, you may also be able to deduct:

- A portion of your rent.
- Costs related to meetings, office supplies, insurance, conferences, tours, workshops, and driving your car for travel writing purposes.
- Professional services such as legal, accounting, consultants, promoters, agents, and sub-contractors.
- Costs to launch and maintain your online presence.

Not Deductible

Deductible expenses must not only be related to your writing project, they also must be reasonable in nature. If you're writing about restaurants, you cannot deduct the cost of your safari, nor should you deduct $750 for a VIP table, unless you are writing an article about VIP bottle service. Other ineligible expenses include:

- Personal travel expenses.
- Anything not paid for by the travel writer/or travel writing company.
- Costs incurred in the days prior to starting work on your writing project or days after you complete it.
- Costs that are in no way related to the production of your article.

"What if I don't sell anything?"

If you can demonstrate that you made a genuine effort to sell your articles, you can generally deduct eligible expenses related to those writing projects. Although your writing projects may not need to be immediately profitable to deduct expenses, you eventually need to turn a profit, otherwise Uncle Sam will lose faith in your entrepreneurial abilities and, eventually, disallow you from making further deductions.

Travel Writing Resource

Lonely Planet's Guide to Travel Writing

BY DON GEORGE

This book is a college degree on travel writing and is one of the first books I read when I started travel writing. It taps into the mind of Lonely Planet's Global Travel Editor, who National Geographic describes as a "legendary travel writer and editor." It covers the basics of good travel writing, along with how to get published and paid.

Part III

Live It, Love It

You made it! Your feet are in the sand, the fresh air is invigorating, and the view is breathtaking. This is how life should be. So now what?

11
Your Wallet: What to Bring, How to Save

Should you lose your wallet abroad, you may not have the luxury of stopping into your bank. A mistake many young travelers make is only traveling with one debit or credit card, leaving them vulnerable if they lose it or it gets damaged. For this reason, you should always have at least two cards each, with enough funds to keep you going if you have to rely solely on one of them.

To save yourself from the panic of losing all your cards at the same time, keep them in separate places, including one on your person and the other hidden in your luggage. In a worst case scenario, if you lose all your cards, you can still make online purchases as long as you know your card number, the expiry date, and the card security code (CSC). Travel agents also have your credit card information on file and can book you a flight or provide your credit card information to you over the phone.

Most credit cards charge a foreign transaction fee, ranging from 1% to 3% of every purchase you make abroad. You can bypass these surcharges by paying for your foreign purchases with a credit card that waives foreign transaction fees. To find the right credit card for you,

I assembled a list of credit cards that offer this benefit under "NO MORE FEES" at breakthetravelbarrier.com.

All banks and currency exchange offices charge currency conversion fees to convert your money into local currency. You can avoid these fees by swapping cash at the day's posted exchange rate with someone you know who lives there. I do this as much as I can, and it works best when visiting friends who moved abroad and return home to visit every year. This way, we avoid currency conversion fees.

When you find yourself having to exchange currency through a financial institution, avoid currency exchange kiosks in airports and malls, as they charge the highest fees. Before leaving on your trip, anticipate how much cash you will need and withdraw it all in one transaction at your local bank.

ATM Fees

Banks routinely charge ATM fees anytime cash is withdrawn by people belonging to other banks, but here are two ways to get around this.

1. There is a little known ATM alliance called the "Global ATM Alliance." The banks that form this alliance waive their ATM fees for users who are with any of the alliance banks. You can find the latest list of Global ATM Alliance members posted at bankofamerica.com. Once you're there, search "Global ATM Alliance."

2. There are a select few bank accounts that waive all ATM fees and will even reimburse you for any ATM fees charged by second-party banks. You can find an up-to-date list of these bank accounts at breakthetravelbarrier.com under "NO MORE FEES."

BE CAREFUL!

Financial systems vary by country and there is no guarantee that a bank you visit abroad will be connected to the global financial network or that your PIN will be compatible with systems you use abroad. Before your trip, ask your home bank if you will be able to access your bank account from your destination.

12
Stay Connected – Without the Bill

I'll never forget my first post-vacation cell phone bill shocker, which came to the tune of $2,108. Fortunately, in the near future, roaming fees will become obsolete, you will have the freedom to connect to any carrier worldwide as easily as you connect to Wi-Fi today, and rates will be comparable to what locals pay.[7]

In the meantime, I'm amazed at how easy it has become to get by strictly using Wi-Fi abroad. Even in underdeveloped countries, free Wi-Fi is increasingly available in airports, touristy areas, restaurants, hotels, cafes, lounges, and libraries. During a trip to the Philippines, I relied on Wi-Fi the entire time and did not feel cut off from the online world at all.

Three Ways to Get Around Roaming Fees:

1. **Deactivate your primary carrier,** along with all roaming capability on your mobile devices, and restrict your online activity to when

you have free Wi-Fi access. If you are visiting friends or family, ask for their Wi-Fi network name and password and connect to their network. When in public, Wi-Fi Finder is a downloadable app that works offline, and it has maps showing where to find free Wi-Fi hotspots.

2. **Unlock your phone** so that it will accept SIM cards from any carrier. Your primary carrier can confirm whether or not your phone is unlocked and will usually unlock it for a nominal a fee. My carrier charged $50 to unlock it, which was well worth the price. The benefit to having an unlocked phone is that it can be used with any SIM card, anywhere in the world, allowing you to get local phone plans at local rates. If you cannot unlock your phone, you can either purchase one locally (basic flip phones sell for as little as $20) or rent an unlocked smartphone for your trip.

3. **Redirect callers to your international number.** To redirect calls from your local number to your international line, you can set up call forwarding to redirect calls to your international number. If your carrier charges call forwarding fees, simply leave a voice message on your main line saying you are out of the country, along with the best way to contact you while you are away.

Roaming Plans

Although wireless carriers are increasingly offering competitive roaming plans, they just aren't good enough when compared to local plans. At the time of this writing, there was one exception: T-Mobile's Simple Choice Plan in the U.S. was (and may still be) offering unlimited text and data in over 100 countries. For the latest list of traveler friendly mobile plans, visit "NO MORE FEES" at breakthetravelbarrier.com.

SIM Cards

You can purchase pre-paid SIM cards at most mobile retail outlets and convenience stores. They come with a local phone number and also cap your financial commitment to what you pre-paid.

If you visit Europe: Le French Mobile offers a multi-lingual pre-paid SIM card at great value and mails the SIM card to you before your trip. Rates are posted on their homepage at lefrenchmobile.com.

For visitors to the U.S.: readysim.com will mail you a SIM card with a phone number that's yours to keep, and will pre-load your plan onto your SIM card. You can also purchase a pre-paid plan online before your trip. If you have already left home, Ready SIM will even mail your SIM card to your U.S. destination (even to a hotel). Rates are comparable to plans offered by local carriers, and you can extend or top up your plan anytime. Roammobility.com is another solution offered by the owners of ReadySim. Roam Mobility is similar to ReadySim but is specifically for Canadians visiting the U.S. and Mexico.

To get the best value for your dollar, stick strictly to data plans. Between Skype, social media, and email, there is no need to pay for talk and text while traveling, when data gives you all three.

Now that you're equipped to get local rates, you can purchase either:

a) A pre-paid SIM card at any convenience store or from operators that mail your SIM card to you prior to your trip.

b) A pre-paid plan.

c) A wireless mobile router or mobile plan through a Mobile Virtual Network Operator (MVNO). To obtain a directory of MVNOs, search "MVNO List" and visit MVNO websites in your country for details.

Keep in Mind

- Each SIM card comes with its own phone number, meaning you will have a different phone number when you when you change your SIM card.

- If there is a chance you will return to a country, you can keep your SIM cards and use them again during your next visit.
- Data plans offer everything that text and talk can do and a lot more.
- By purchasing pre-paid SIM cards, your financial commitment is capped to what you pre-pay.

Internet Charges

Many hotels and resorts charge as much as $20 a day for internet access, and an upscale hotel was once caught charging $236 Euros a day for in-room internet. On top of that, hotels and resorts increasingly tack on additional surcharges for connecting more than a set number of devices simultaneously from one room.

You can try to get out of expensive in-room internet fees by complain at check-out time that your connection was interrupted throughout your stay and was too slow for you to work on. Until the day comes when everyone does this, there is a chance your fee will get waived.

If you need to be online, do not take a cruise! Internet fees can range from $35 to $60 an hour and more! If you absolutely must go online while on a cruise, T-Mobile partners with a number of cruise ships to offer mobile plans, and you can browse a directory of cruise ships that offer T-Mobile's cruise ship plan in T-Mobile's cruise ship services directory.

Hacking Airport Wi-Fi

If an airport doesn't offer free Wi-Fi and you can't get into the executive lounge, the following tip has scored me free Wi-Fi a handful of times. Look for a restaurant or sitting area next to an airport lounge, and search for unsecured network connections. I was doing this as I wrote these words from Stefani's Tuscany Cafe, next to the United Club in Chicago O'Hare Airport.

Surfers Beware

When using public Wi-Fi networks, your privacy is at risk because hackers can see what you do on the internet and steal any information that you type or display online.

To protect yourself:

- Validate that the Wi-Fi connection is authentic (hackers often set up fake networks with seemingly legitimate names).
- Use applications like VPN (Virtual Private Network) and Easysurf, when connecting to public networks.
- If you don't have any of the above safeguards in place, the rule of thumb when using public hot spots is not to type or view anything you wouldn't want a stranger to see.

Alternative Wi-Fi Solutions

Destination	Solution
> 600,000 hotspots in most major cities	Get online access with Boingo for a few dollars per month. Remember to cancel your account between trips, as Boingo has a monthly auto-renewal policy.
> 100 Countries	IRoam global roaming offers solutions for as little as $10 a month and unlimited internet access for up to 8 devices simultaneously.
> 40 Countries	Globalgig.com sells mobile hotspot devices, starting at $30 a month, that work in over 40 countries for up to 5 devices at a time.
Canadians visiting the U.S.	roammobility.com offers visitors to the U.S. a Liberty mobile hot spot device you can use to connect your devices for pennies per MG.

13
Finding Inexpensive Things to Do

The fastest route is rarely the most scenic or the most exciting. That's why, during a vacation in Venice, I gave myself the task of finding each major bridge without the help of any maps. It gave me a reason to talk to people, I allowed myself to get side tracked along the way, and I rejoiced every time I found a bridge. The journey was more satisfying than finding the bridges themselves. I now seek to do this on every trip, as follows:

1. **Find a purpose that forces you to get out there:** Whether you decide to see the Seven Wonders of the World, attend all the Olympics, or visit every Hard Rock Café in the world. These goals give you a reason to get out there.

2. **Allow yourself to get side tracked:** Know that your most amazing moments will often occur unexpectedly.

3. **It's okay to splurge:** When you have good travel-savvy habits, it's fine to splurge, every once in a while, and to pay fair value for something you long for. Just as with a diet, you need to

treat yourself every so often, to keep yourself from binging. My binge is to occasionally stay in hotels with rooftop pools atop high rises; I get excited at the thought of swimming high above the Marina Bay Sands in Singapore or the Shanghai high rise seen in the movie Skyfall.

Finding Inexpensive Excursions

Here is a story about a savvy travel bug named Sally and how she packed her schedule during a trip to Phoenix with inexpensive things to do.

Two weeks prior to her trip, Sally ran two Google searches. Her first search was for "Phoenix weekly events newsletters." She learned that Downtown Phoenix Vitality publishes a weekly events newsletter, and she signed up for it. In the days prior to her trip, Sally received a Downtown Phoenix Vitality newsletter, which is how she learned of:

- A Saturday morning public run that finishes at a local market.
- Community yoga taking place in Civic Space Park.
- A folk music festival at 5th and Garfield.

Sally's second online search was for Phoenix's tourist information center. She saved the address in Evernote under "Phoenix – To Dos" and sent that information to "21March11am@followupthen.com." Sally then went to Ticketmaster to see if there were any concerts or shows that would interest her and learned that Nick Carter would be performing during her visit.

Before purchasing anything, Sally tried something else that most tourists overlook. She regularly receives newsletters from groupon.com, livingsocial.com, and slickdeals.net, which offer local coupons for upwards of 40% to 50% off everything from hotels, restaurants, spas, and golf to activities and excursions in her hometown. Sally changed her hometown in her e-couponing accounts to Phoenix, and she started receiving e-coupons she could use to get discounts during her vacation in Phoenix.

Before making any decisions about what to do, Sally visited viator.com to find the best things to do in Phoenix and also read reviews and recommendations from other travelers who have visited Phoenix at tripntale.com.

Once in Phoenix, Sally partook in the Saturday morning run then stopped into a bookstore for her morning latte. She spent a few minutes browsing the bookstore when, to her delight, she found two local guidebooks titled "Best Local Hiking Trails" and "Best Restaurants as Voted by the City." She bought both and continued on her way. She received an email reminder to visit the tourist information center, which happened to be on route to "Yoga in the Park." Once at the tourist center, she met friendly staff and found a treasure trove of information about local excursions and events. She pinpointed a few that interested her and continued on to "Yoga in the Park."

Sally's story illustrates how simple it is to find inexpensive things to do while traveling.

Inexpensive Excursions

You will be surprised to learn that admission to some of the world's great festivals is free. For instance, admission into the Oktoberfest grounds and tents in Munich is free, and the Taj Mahal offers free admission on Fridays, for those who visit to pray. The following are a collection of ways I saved money, while on the road, that you can use, too.

City Explorer Pass

By purchasing an Explorer Pass, you can visit many major attractions in a city for upwards of 40% off. Passes are available at smartdestinations.com and sometimes from Costco.com, and you can customize your card to only pay for attractions that interest you. Another way Costco members can save even more is to visit a

Costco store at their destination and purchase $100 gift cards for local restaurants and activities, which are often sold for $80. Let's say you're going on a ski vacation in Lake Tahoe, the local Costco sells discounted ski, spa and hotel, and restaurant vouchers for $80, entitling you to $100 in services. On top of that, executive Costco members get 2% cash back on Costco purchases, which can get you a $100 voucher for $78.40.

National Parks

Parks like Oregon's Ecola State Park and Alberta's Banff National Park only charge fees to those who leave their cars unattended in the park. You can visit these parks for free by viewing them from your car and not leaving your vehicle unattended, except at service stations and rest stops. If you decide to wander from your vehicle without a park pass, keep your car within sight, or don't leave it for long so that ticketers do not find your car unattended without a park permit.

There are a number of days each year that all 401 National Parks in the U.S. are free to visit. For a list of National Parks that are free to visit, go to nps.gov and lookup "Free Parks."

Keep Fit while on the Run

Don't fall into the trap of eating too much, drinking too much, and sleeping too little while traveling. When you take your workout abroad, whether it's running along a mountaintop overlooking Copacabana Beach, Paris' Seine River, or the Mediterranean coast, you can nostalgically recapture the magic of those moments, long after you leave, while running at home. Even if you don't usually exercise, what better time to start than when you're traveling and have the time to do it? If you want to see more in less time, what better way to do it than to jog or ride a bike? Many of the world's busiest, happiest, and most successful people thrive by making exercise part of their daily life. So find a way to make it happen, and get those endorphins flowing!

Discounted Massages and Workouts

Many health benefit plans entitle you to claim expenses for massages that are provided by registered massage therapists. Some plans have restrictions, as to what you can claim, so ask your benefits provider to check the specific terms and conditions.

If you want to work out, many spas also have gyms, and you can leverage your spa benefits to also work out at no extra cost. I have had many free workouts, by offering to buy a smoothie in lieu of paying a drop-in fee. You can also get inexpensive workouts in the U.S. by using a GPS-enabled app called gymsurfing to find nearby gyms with drop-in fees starting at $5. Here is another way I earned a free workout:

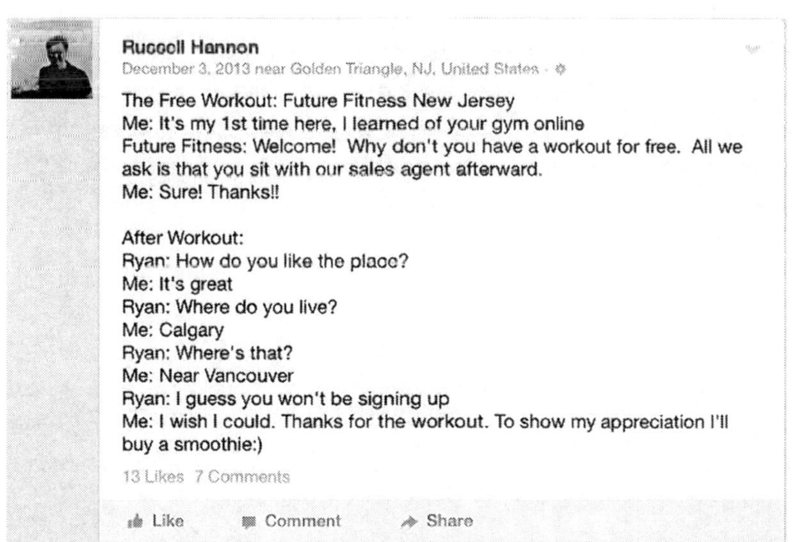

Russell Hannon
December 3, 2013 near Golden Triangle, NJ, United States

The Free Workout: Future Fitness New Jersey
Me: It's my 1st time here, I learned of your gym online
Future Fitness: Welcome! Why don't you have a workout for free. All we ask is that you sit with our sales agent afterward.
Me: Sure! Thanks!!

After Workout:
Ryan: How do you like the place?
Me: It's great
Ryan: Where do you live?
Me: Calgary
Ryan: Where's that?
Me: Near Vancouver
Ryan: I guess you won't be signing up
Me: I wish I could. Thanks for the workout. To show my appreciation I'll buy a smoothie:)

13 Likes 7 Comments

Like Comment Share

Free Shower Access

A free shower is always as close to you as the next public beach, pool, campground, fitness center, or truck stop. To get free access, my trick is to politely offer to purchase food in exchange for being granted access to their facilities.

If you fancy something more upscale, a friend of mine strutted into Claridge's hotel in London with his sandals in hand and abruptly interrupted a clerk by asking, "Which way to the pool?" Upon being pointed in the right direction, he asked, "Do I need a key? My parents have them." Like magic, the clerk handed him a key to the spa, no questions asked. The brilliance wasn't in what he did as much as how he did it. By acting like a guest, the clerk assumed he was one.

Free Bag Stowage

If you need a secure place to store your luggage, some airports allow you to check your bags as much as 24 hours in advance. I once did this using the airport express check-in in downtown Vienna so I could then explore the city without my bags. You can also check your bags into stowage at hotels, casinos, and museums. I have taken advantage of this at more hotels and casinos than I can count.

Libraries

Make a point of knowing where the municipal library is, as you can often read newspapers for free and get free internet access. Some libraries, such as Seattle's Public Library, have such extravagant architecture that they are tourist attractions themselves.

Spa Nap Rooms

It happened half by accident …

After a night out in Vegas, I stopped into the spa for some much needed rest and relaxation. That's when I stumbled upon a dimly lit serenity room with semi-private napping beds. Within seconds of flopping onto a napping bed, I was fast asleep and, when I woke five hours later, I joked that I could have saved myself the cost of a room by going straight to the spa that morning. "Hmmmm …"

Fast forward nine months. I was organizing a bachelor party and arrived in Vegas a day before the guys. It was time to put my theory to the test:

10:00 p.m.: I split a cab with people I met on the plane, and we agreed to meet up that night for drinks.

10:30 p.m.: I checked my suitcase into stowage (free) and took a walk on the strip.

11:30 p.m.: I met up with the gang I met on the flight, and we toasted to Friday night in Vegas, before going out for a night on the town.

5:00 a.m.: Breakfast at Denny's.

6:00 a.m.: The spa opened its doors, and I was the only one in line when I signed up for a full-day access pass ($42).

6:15 a.m.: With the whole spa to myself, I plunged into the hot tub, then put on a plush white robe and flip flops and proceeded to the nap room.

3:00 p.m.: I woke nearly eight hours later with a big yawn and a stretch, before taking another dip in the hot tub and retrieving my bag as the guys arrived.

Any time I fly a red eye and need a nap in the morning, I look for spas with nap rooms. Spas are great places to recharge the batteries and, besides, what hotel would ever think they have guests sleeping in their spas instead of a room?

Free Airport Parking

Most large airports have charter airlines and private carriers nearby. Through my business travels, I noticed that many private hangars lack parking controls so I also park there for my personal trips and take a $5 taxi ride to the airport. Savvy Las Vegans have a similar trick: they forgo the cost of airport parking by parking at the nearby Hard Rock hotel then taking a short taxi ride to the airport.

How to Skip Lines and Door Fees

What if there was one thing you could say that would magically convince a doorman to let you in over a hundred others? Here are three:

1. Approach the doorman and say, "Sorry, I know you're crazy busy. I live with _____ (make up a name) at bar number two who has my house keys and is expecting me. Can I go in to get my keys?"

2. Walk straight in through the exit and, when you are stopped, respond with, "I just walked out 5 seconds ago, but my friends didn't follow me." Then point at a group of people and say, "They're right there."

3. I've hung on to my business cards from a summer job I had in college, as a promotional beer representative. Although I have not tried this in a few years, doormen would always let

me in when I showed it to them and said, "Hi, I stocked the fridges this morning, and the manager invited me to stop in tonight for a drink."

Free Tour Gone Awry

As luck would have it, I arrived at the world's oldest medieval monastery two minutes after the last tour of the day had departed. As we left, a group following a lead monk walked by us so we seized the moment and joined along. After a few minutes and receiving some unwelcoming glares, someone whispered that this was a private tour so we played the naive tourist card and gracefully turned back. The problem was that the gate from which we entered had locked behind us, and we could not get out! With no other option, we returned to the group and were unable to ask for assistance as the monk was narrating the tour. Out of respect to the monk, everyone stayed quiet and, in the end, we got the tour for free—albeit in a slightly unsettling fashion.

If you have stories or savvy tricks and tips that have saved you money while traveling, share them and learn from others in the Travel Bug Forum at breakthetravelbarrier.com.

Did You Know?

You can recoup many of the taxes you pay on retail purchases in Europe?

The European Union (E.U.) has a program that entitles visitors from non E.U. countries to recoup the value added tax (VAT) paid on physical goods purchased and returned with you to your home country (consumed goods and services do not qualify). Most countries set a minimum dollar value for qualifying purchases, and the amount varies from $50 to $200 or $300, except for Ireland, where purchases of any amount are eligible.

The process for recouping VAT is so confusing and ill-defined that only a few qualifying purchases are ever successfully claimed.

Lucky for you, the following steps show you how to be one of the few visitors to Europe to recoup every eligible VAT dollar paid.

First, the program is voluntary and retailers have the option of choosing whether or not to participate. Before you purchase anything, it is important that you ask the retailer if it participates in the VAT refund program. If so:

1. Show the clerk your passport at the point of purchase. You will have to pay the tax up front, but the clerk will complete a VAT refund form and provide it to you.

2. Before you leave the store:

    a. Many VAT refund service providers have kiosks in major airports and can issue your refund as you depart the country. Ask the retailer for the name of any VAT refund service providers they partner with so that you can look for them at your departing airport.

    b. If you leave the country by ground or cannot find the VAT refund service provider at your departing airport, you will need to claim your refund by mail. For that reason, ask the retailer for a pre-posted envelop with the VAT refund provider's mailing address.

3. Before submitting your VAT refund form, customs must stamp it before you depart the country. As you leave the country, show the customs agent your VAT refund form, receipt, and passport, and have the item with you in case the customs agent asks to see it. If you are departing by air, you will need to locate the customs kiosk in the airport.

4. Once customs stamps your VAT refund form, you can collect your refund. If you are at an airport, ask the customs agent to direct you to the VAT refund service provider that your retailer referred you to.

If you cannot collect your refund prior to departure, use the post-dated envelope provided to you by your retailer to submit your stamped VAT refund claim by mail. Send it in as quickly as possible, as there are deadlines after which VAT refund claims are no longer honored. When submitting claims by mail, don't be surprised if it takes a few months to get your refund.

Even when you follow all the rules, you may occasionally run into the odd problem. In October 2011, I submitted a claim for masquerade masks I purchased in Venice and, despite doing all of the above, I have yet to receive my refund.

Shopping

Shopping can turn your trip into a budget buster. There are only two circumstances that justify buying things while traveling:

1. You have a practical need for it.
2. You know you will eventually buy it anyway, AND it is cheaper to buy abroad than at home.

Don't buy gifts while traveling just because you feel you should. You really only need to bring gifts back in two cases: for a significant other and for your kids. That said, you may have a soft spot, just as I do for my nephews and nieces, and, by keeping a creative hat on, there are all kinds of things they will love that don't cost much.

There's no need to avoid tourist traps, just don't shop in them. Many of the souvenirs and trinkets there are not as unique as you may think. You can find the same trinkets anywhere from Olympic National Park to Acadia National Park, and the only difference is the name of the place inscribed on them.

Finally, if you are traveling with kids, tell them at the outset that they can only get one or two items during the whole trip.

14
Disaster Prevention
Taking Care of Number One

What could possibly go wrong?

You can make all the right moves and still get wiped out by a black swan. Black swans are unpredictable and unlikely disasters that have devastating consequences:

- In the U.K. alone, more than 74,000 people are left without a vacation they pre-paid for, each year, when travel operators go bankrupt.
- On the 4th of July weekend in Panama Beach, Florida, a parasail detached from a boat, leaving two girls to drift into a high-rise condo building.
- During a Christmas holiday on the Mayan Riviera, a hotel balcony collapsed, and the hospital demanded $2,500 in cash before treating a seriously injured woman. To literally add insult to injury, the hotel turned around and charged her thousands of dollars to repair the balcony!

Although you cannot predict when a black swan like this will occur, there are things you can do to protect yourself from the fallout:

1. Always travel with enough means to get home. If you are on a budget or are uncertain of your plans, get an open-end return ticket.

2. Pay for trips either through a travel agent or using a credit card so that you can recoup any paid services that a travel operator fails to provide.

3. Before traveling abroad, look up the address and contact information of your Embassy at your destination. The Travel Safe Pro app has an Embassy directory with emergency numbers by country.

4. Don't travel without global medical insurance. Even if you don't think you need it, get it. The person who lost an arm in a shark attack didn't think they would need it, either. Having global medical insurance can sometimes make the difference between life and death or financial ruin. But, before purchasing global medical insurance:

    - Check your employer's medical coverage to see what health coverage you have when traveling abroad.

    - Many credit cards offer travel insurance benefits, if you pay for your travel with it.

    - If you're a student under age 25, check to see if you are covered under your parents' policy.

If you have exhausted the above options and do not have adequate global medical insurance, you can buy comprehensive travel insurance for as little as $30 per trip. Worldnomads.com offers travel insurance to people from just about anywhere visiting anywhere. Simply provide your country of residence, destination, and dates and you will be traveling. If the day ever comes that you need it, you will be glad you got it.

5. When you travel, things naturally get misplaced, and phones occasionally break. That's why it's important to make copies of important travel documents, including your passport and insurance, and that you have:
    - Originals on your person.
    - Photocopies in your luggage.
    - Scanned copies accessible online.

6. Protect your possessions:
    - To reduce the chances of losing everything at once, keep your cash and credit cards in separate places.
    - Lock your luggage, and keep it secured or in sight.
    - If you sleep on a bus, train, or in a hostel, make sure important things cannot be taken or accessed without waking you.
    - When visiting underdeveloped countries, keep your money, smart phone, and jewelry out of sight.

7. Stay safe:
    - Remain constantly aware of your surroundings.
    - Don't divulge sensitive personal information to strangers.

- Do not flash anything that could tempt opportunists.
- Don't wander alone at night or without knowing where the unsafe areas are.
- Never cross borders with people you just met or carry anything across a border for someone else.
- Turn down drinks offered from strangers that are not served directly to you, and disregard drinks that you leave unattended.
- Expand your vocabulary beyond "cerveza por favor" to include "no," "stop," and "help" in the local language.
- Keep a friend or family member back home posted on where you are.
- A cell phone is a safety tool and not just a luxury. Chapter 12 shows you how to stay connected abroad—without the bill.
- Inquire through credible sources whether there are laws you need to know or areas to avoid.

8. Familiarize yourself with local laws and cultural sensitivities so that you don't unknowingly cross any lines. Your official government website will have a travel advisory page that you can use to research destinations and read about local laws you should be aware of. For instance, many people don't know that in Singapore you can get fined for:

    - Smoking in public ($150).
    - Jaywalking, chewing gum, spitting in public, eating on the transit system ($375).
    - Littering ($225). *The court sends third-time offenders to clean the streets with bibs that say, "I'm a litterer."

- Failing to flush public toilets after use.
- Possessing pornography.

Punishable by Death

- Unlawful discharge of a firearm, even if no one is hurt.
- Import, export, manufacture, or possession of drugs exceeding quantities measured in grams.

In the Middle East, police can arrest or deport you for offending public decency, which they define as:

- Being too friendly.
- Speaking directly to a woman in the presence of her male companion.
- Kissing in public.
- Women staring into the eyes of a married man.

Cultural Sensitivities

If anyone ever appears to be offended by something you did, do the triple A: Acknowledge your error, Apologize, then Act to correct the issue. If the offended person is drinking, remove yourself from the situation so that things do not escalate.

9. Stay healthy:

    Before you travel, find out whether you should be vaccinated against regional illnesses. The website for the U.S. Centers for Disease Control and Prevention (cdc.gov) has a travel section that posts health advisories and offers preventative recommendations by destination.

TIP: You wouldn't believe how dirty many planes are. Elbows often have small abrasions that can serve as entry points for bacteria. For that reason, consider wearing long sleeve shirts when you fly.

To protect yourself against foodborne illness:

- Make sure your food is thoroughly cooked.
- Eat local yogurt when you arrive, to accustom your stomach to the local bacteria.
- Avoid dirty restaurants as well as fruits and salads, which are sometimes not washed in fresh water.
- Don't drink tap or well water, as they naturally have germs and bacteria that your body may not handle well. Consider getting a SteriPEN, which is a portable water purifier that emits UV light to kill microbes in water.

10. Prevent identity theft:

    A Norton cybercrime report showed that one in six people fell victim to cybercrime in 2012. This means you are likely to fall victim to cybercrime once every six years. To minimize the chances of being part of this statistic, take the following precautions before you connect to Wi-Fi hot spots:

- Hackers often create fake hot spots with names that look legitimate, and they can see everything you do, once you connect. When you connect to a public network, always ask an employee for the official Wi-Fi network name.
- Get VPN (virtual private network) or Easysurf to keep your online activity secure.
- Restrict your online activity and don't type or view anything you wouldn't want a stranger sitting next to you to see.

Planes, Trains & Scams

There are three inescapable things in life: Death, Taxes, and Scams. Every year, hundreds of millions of travelers fall victim to scams. Here are some of the cleverest and most notorious ones that can bleed your wallet dry and even land you in a hospital. In the case of the Agra food poisoning scam, insurance companies found a restaurant that was deliberately poisoning tourists and sending them to a doctor, who split the insurance payouts with them. To the best of my knowledge, this scam was disbanded, but there are other cases of similar scams in various parts of the world. Here is a list of extreme travel scams you should be aware of:

The Black Widow Scam

In Colombia, a black widow—a sultry woman—approaches a man in a lounge or nightclub and insists on going home with him. When they arrive, she incapacitates him with a date-rape drug and robs him. Common drugs used include:

- Rohypnol or "Roofies," which are tasteless and dilute quickly into drinks.

- Burundanga and scopolamine (also known as Devil's Breath and the zombie drug) are plant-based drugs, mostly grown in Colombia, that incapacitate people within minutes of being inhaled or ingested. Victims remain conscious and coherent, but they lose their free will and have been known to blindly hand over their possessions and empty their bank accounts. Once the drug wears off, people do not remember anything.

Mazo Scooter Scam

Guys, what do you do when in Mazo and beautiful ladies playfully pull up on scooters, inviting you to join them? You say no! Organized gangs dispatch young women to lure affluent tourists to a home, where they rob you.

Pickpockets

Pike Place Market, Seattle, WA, October 2012: While waiting in line at Starbucks, I noticed someone trying to make eye contact with me, who suddenly ran up and asked if I wanted to hear a funny joke. Without even thinking, my hands dropped down over my pockets and my head swivelled; I found out that he was talking to someone he knew, who happened to be standing behind me. In this case, it turned out I was fine, but I am always skeptical when strangers seemingly try too hard to get my attention:

- Carry your valuables in your front or inside pockets.
- Remain alert for suspicious activity happening around you.
- If you have valuables in a bag, keep it on your front side, where you can see it.

Taxi Scams

Once a taxi driver realizes you have no idea where you are, there is a chance you may get taken for a ride. I once had a driver take me on a scenic tour around the coastline of Nice, France, when my hotel was, in fact, directly across from the airport. The driver was so smooth that I almost didn't mind the tour, which ran up my meter. I called him the "Nice, Nice Scammer."

A friend of mine hopped into a taxi in Vietnam and handed the driver a printout with her hotel details. Thirty minutes later, her taxi pulled over next to police, and the driver abruptly got out, unloaded her luggage, and started yelling. With her hotel nowhere in sight and two policemen approaching, the driver put his hand out. Confused and unable to speak the language, she read between the lines, paid him, and was left stranded without the faintest idea of what to do next.

Be leery of drivers who insist on taking you somewhere other than your destination. In some places, it is common for establishments to pay taxis kickbacks per drop off.

Illegal Taxis

If you unknowingly take a ride in an illegal taxi, you could suddenly find yourself being exploited. Illegal taxis are unlicensed, unscreened, and uninsured cars that lurk around airports and touristy areas. Some have rigged meters, and others have no meter at all.

The La Paz taxi scam is an extreme example, in which scammers driving fake taxis offer rides to La Paz and encounter staged hijackings or police checks along the way; passengers are typically threatened and detained (sometimes for days) before being robbed.

Anytime you find yourself in unfamiliar territory, stick to taxis in officially monitored pickup lanes. Avoid cars that do not have a radio dispatch, official registration, and a posted taxi service telephone number. As a precaution, you can call the phone number on the taxi, before getting in, to verify that it is authentic. If anything has you feeling uncomfortable or unsure, do not get in.

To protect yourself from compromising situations, while riding in taxis:

- Do not accept rides from drivers soliciting you in unusual places or ways.
- Stick to official taxi pickup lines.
- Keep your luggage with you so that, if something happens, you can toss a few bills to the driver and jump out with all your things.
- Clearly communicate exactly where you are going and how you want to get there. This includes the name of your destination, its exact address, and which major streets to take.
- Insist on agreeing to a price up front. Ask the driver to write your destination on a piece of paper, with the price, and hand it to you.
- Make a few comments that suggest you know the area and have been there before.

When a Taxi Driver Overcharges You:

- Leave the agreed upon cash on the seat, and calmly get out.
- Take a picture of the car and driver, if you can.
- Get the taxi license number or the license plate number.

Be Careful!

Pedi cab drivers (three-wheeled rickshaw runners) have been known to offer prices up front and later insist that the offered price is "per person."

Counterfeit Tickets

Event tickets are easy to counterfeit. The only way to protect yourself is to only purchase tickets from official organizations associated with the event. If you buy tickets from scalpers, arrange it so you can validate your ticket at the box office or at the gate, before you pay.

"Free" Tours

In dense tourist areas like the Forbidden City and Tiananmen Square, scammers are paid commissions by vendors for bringing tourists in. Be on the lookout for free or inexpensive tours, where these scammers lure you into an endless string of overpriced markets and lame acts. Red flags can include overcrowded or poorly maintained tour buses and random people selling tours on the street. To protect yourself, book tours through official companies and ask detailed questions before you book.

The "You Won a Free Trip" Scam

Can you recall the first time you received a call saying you won a free trip, and all you had to do was pay $400 or call a 1-900 number? Don't bite on these sorts of claims.

Credit Card Scams

Some scammers eavesdrop as people check into their hotel. They later call their room, claiming to be the front desk and saying that, due to a technical issue, they need to ask for their credit card information again. During a trip in London, someone somehow got my credit card number and used it to book a flight from Singapore to Kuala Lumpur in Australian currency. I reported it, and my credit card company refunded me, but I never did figure out how my number was compromised.

To Protect Yourself:

- Don't allow vendors to print your credit card details using old-school carbon copied printers.
- Keep your credit card out of the vendor's hands and handle your card yourself. Fraudsters swipe credit cards through machines that copy the data, and they later clone the card.

Some eavesdropping scammers go as far as approaching the front desk, claiming to be you, saying they forgot their key in their room, and asking for another one. Naive clerks sometimes fall for this and hand the robber a room key. The robber then cleans out your room, while you're out.

Street Entertainers

The world's great tourist attractions all have one thing in common: They are all filled with street entertainers. Whether it's Elmo in Time Square, card games on the street, or children offering you flowers, don't accept anything without first asking outright if they will charge you for it.

Bar Tabs

Never hand over your credit card to start a tab. Pay as you go to protect yourself from getting overcharged. It's important to always keep track of what you order and what the prices are. Restaurants in touristy areas have occasionally been found to have "tourist menus" with inflated prices.

Bike/Scooter Rental Scam

In this scam, bicycle rental companies charge a deposit and then send someone to follow you. When you leave your bicycle unattended, the person uses a spare key to unlock your bicycle and takes it.

Counterfeit Money

In countries where money can easily be counterfeited, some retailers are notorious for the "bait-and-switch," where they quickly swap legitimate bills with fake ones and return the fake ones to unsuspecting tourists, asking them to pay with a different bill. Then, they scam the tourist a second time, by issuing them counterfeit money as change.

Deceiving Ads

A free flight to Jamaica sounds great, until you read the fine print that says, "When you book for 11 nights at $79 per person + tax and resort fees. Assume quadruple occupancy. Free flight only applies to one person one-way and does not cover airline surcharges, including but not limited to taxes, surcharges, baggage check-in fees, airport improvement, and transfer fees."

At Niagara Falls, I once read a sign saying, "$51 Rooms" and walked in, only to be handed a piece of piece of paper with the number "$79" written on it. My response was, "Let's go outside, I'd like you to see what your sign says," to which he responded, with a straight face, "$51 is for stays of seven consecutive nights or more."

"Bon Voyage!" Said the Burglar

While you are away, there are also scammers trying to rob you at home. I returned from a trip in February 2013 to find my car had been broken into at the airport; my garage opener and vehicle registration had been stolen. Had I not lived in a condo, the thieves would have had direct access to my home through the garage.

Protect Yourself

Prior to traveling to an unfamiliar destination, run a Google search to see what scams are prevalent there. Once you are aware of prevalent scams, you can take steps to protect yourself. If you have fallen victim to a scam, share your story in the TRAVEL BUG forum at breakthet-ravelbarrier.com.

15
Pulling It All Together

Hong Kong, here we come!

After years of putting off a trip to Hong Kong, imagine finding yourself finally eating noodles from the peak of Victoria Park. As you stare out into the city, you are completely mesmerized by the sun setting behind Hong Kong's breathtaking skyline. In that moment, you think back to all the times you passed it up in favor of less expensive destinations. You can now spend two weeks there, for a fraction of what it would have cost to visit two years ago. Here is how the Dream Travel Plan makes this possible:

People

Thirty minutes until show time …

It was a Friday evening in Leicester Square, and we had a show to catch. As I hurried to finish my fish and chips, I chugged my beer while I explained to Kyla the concept of the Dream Travel Plan. The moment I mentioned to her that I had been holding off on visiting Hong Kong in favor of less expensive destinations, Kyla jumped off her chair, leaned forward, and shouted over the raucous crowd, saying her best friend had just moved to Hong Kong for work. She insisted that we get in touch and was certain we would get along great. That same week, a childhood friend sent me a note from the Philippines saying hi and reminding me that I had to get over there to visit him. Poof! From out of nowhere, I suddenly had two people I could stay with in Southeast Asia.

Means

By planning your trip months out, you can often earn enough points to fly to your destination. The "FUND YOUR TRAVELS" section of breakthetravelbarrier.com has a list of credit cards that offer sign-up bonuses you can redeem for free flights, with no annual fee your first year. If you are relying on points earned through purchases, you can stockpile points without buying anything, by following the instructions on page 46.

Another way you can get a great deal on a flight is to follow the instructions in scenario #1 of the Fast Tracker on page 142. It shows you how to beat the best online fare, and it once got me a round trip flight to Asia for $875, whereas the woman sitting next to me paid double that.

To avoid paying foreign transaction fees for out of country purchases charged to a credit card, pay for all your international purchases with a credit card that waives foreign transaction fees. Any time you can, swap cash with people you are visiting at the day's exchange rate, to keep currency conversion fees to a minimum.

Hong Kong hosts an annual fundraising marathon for a number of charities. By running in that marathon, you can launch a crowdfunding campaign, contribute the donations to any of the affiliated charities, and use those donations to partially offset your travel costs to run in the marathon.

Since this fundraiser could make for an interesting story, you can earn a few dollars by pitching this story to local newspapers, magazines, and websites, using the Travel Writing Sales Solicitation template at the back of this book (Appendix C). If you do this, ask your tax advisor which expenses are deductible.

A month prior to the trip, run a Google search of things to do at your destination. Let's say you learn of a great restaurant with an amazing view, a great way to remember this restaurant is to send an email with the restaurant details to "daymonthtime@followupthen.com." For example, "13july10am@followupthen.com" will arrive in your inbox on that exact date and time with the details you want to be reminded of. Another thing you can do is save the information about that restaurant in Evernote with the tag "Hong Kong – To Dos."

Knowledge

To save money while sightseeing in Hong Kong, an iVenture card can get you into many of the city's major activities and attractions for nearly 40% off.

To get around roaming fees, make sure your phone is unlocked, and bring or purchase a pre-paid SIM card with a data-only plan at rates comparable to what locals pay. With Skype and social media, you can get by on a data plan and forgo talk and text plans. If your phone is locked, you can purchase an inexpensive phone at your destination or rely on free Wi-Fi, which is increasingly available in hotels, restaurants, cafes, libraries, train stations, and airports.

By staying with locals, you can steer clear of many of many scams that tourists are susceptible to. Had I not been with my good friend Luc while in Southeast Asia, I would have surely been scammed a number of times. Luc doesn't fall for any scams; he's the master and knows how to handle them all.

Creativity

You can often get free workouts by going to gyms with locals who have a membership there and saying you are visiting for the first time. When traveling in the U.S., gymsurfing is an app that shows you nearby gyms with daily drop-in fees for as little as $5 per workout.

If there are multiple places you want so see during your trip, save yourself the cost of multiple flights by booking a flight to the furthest destination with extended stopovers in nearer destinations. Since you cannot book flights with extended stopovers online, book such routes directly over the telephone, as agents can do this for you and telephone booking fees cost significantly less than change fees.

Flexibility

By steering clear of committing to a fixed schedule, I will be able to take advantage of unexpected opportunities, as they arise, without worry or restrictions.

Adaptability

By adapting to inevitable minor nuisances that are bound to occur while traveling, you can keep your cool and not let the small stuff ruin your vacation, such as not being able to find a retailer that sells SIM cards.

Summary

That momentous moment in the Leicester Square proved to me that the Dream Travel Plan works, and it works better than all the other travel advice out there. Unlike one-off tips and tricks that tell you where to go and what to do, the Dream Travel Plan pulls the best travel resources together so you can leverage them all. This is all that stands between you and the world. Now that you have it, it's time to live your dream.

Maybe I'll see you in Hong Kong!

Closing Remarks

The more you travel, the more it changes you. Your family and friends will notice that you've picked up new tastes and have broader perspectives. They will also find you to be one of the most interesting people to speak with!

As you overcome the financial barriers to travel, a new dilemma will emerge: "The more you get, the more you will want." I call it the traveler's dilemma.

Every spring, the Fairmont Banff Springs hotel puts on the Super Bowl of wine and food festivals, in an opulent ball room worthy of royalty. This year, it just so happens that that the festival fell on my birthday, and I came by a bottle of scotch bottled 37 years ago to the day, which happened to be the exact day I was born! Not surprisingly, a sipping size portion cost fifteen times more than other drinks, but it was the finest scotch I ever had.

My birthday shot reminded me of many places I have traveled to. It was amazingly good, it didn't last long and, once it was done, that was it. I relate this to travel because there are more wonders in the world than you will ever be able to experience. Life only lasts so long, and you can only be in one place at a time. Of all the places you visit, you will only ever return to a handful of them and of those, only a select few can ever become a "home away from home."

You will often have to settle for a small slice of the many wonderful people you meet and places you experience, before moving on. Often, you won't realize how precious a moment is until after it has passed. You can't have it all, but now you can travel more, stay longer, spend less, and live a more fulfilling life.

Make Your Mark in the World

> "Be the change that you wish to see in the world."
> – Mahatma Gandhi

When the system you live under fails to keep up with innovation, it keeps you from reaping the full benefits of that innovation. Imagine wearing the same clothes every day, for five years. That's exactly what many of us do with our cars and our homes. The entire ownership model came about before mass commercial aviation, when people spent most of their lives in one place. It's as out-dated as the flip phone, as it fails to provide for the needs of the emerging travel lifestyle.

Imagine living in a truly global world that facilitates freedom of movement. What if:

- Instead of owning one home, you could own the right to occupy any of a number of homes, all over the world, and could transfer to another dwelling for a nominal fee?

- Instead of buying a car, you could buy the rights to have one car in your possession at all times, from a global pool of cars. You could choose from packages that allow you to swap cars a set number of times a year and have access to a mix of car classes. For instance, you could purchase a package that entitles you to a convertible for four weekends, a luxury SUV for a week, and a mid-size sedan the rest of the year.

Such an ownership model would facilitate a new form of travel lifestyle unlike anything before it.

Your Chance to Change the World

Here are three things you can do to make the world a better place:

1. Pass forward the lessons you learned from this book so your friends and family can also benefit. By inspiring and empowering them, you can reap the rewards of ultra-economical travel together.

2. Take a stance against one thing that makes travel costs prohibitive. Whether it's deceiving advertising, ridiculous surcharges, exploitive roaming fees, or tourist visas, form a group of likeminded people, and make your collective voice heard.

3. In this era of unprecedented change and evolution, there have never been more ways to travel for the local cost of living. If you are in a position of public influence or have the ability to contribute to economic reform, seek to reform systems that can liberate the travel lifestyle.

In the words of Abraham Maslow, "We fear to become that which we can glimpse in our most perfect moments." Bringing this book to you involved overcoming fears of my own. The same way I found the courage to ski over the edge of Panorama Mountain, I found inspiration in a number of young, revolutionary authors who convinced me you don't need to be a celebrity to publish a book or be an astronaut to make a difference in the world. You just need to know how to reach out in ways nobody else has.

Millions of people are traveling free every day; make sure that on some of those days, you're among us. No more settling for the going rate. Finished with asking others for travel tips. Done are the days of waiting for when you can travel more. The world is yours. I wish you all that is great, and I hope to hear from you along the way

Bon voyage, Mon Ami!

RUSSELL HANNON

It Is Now Your Turn

Our journey does not end here. The pages in this book come to life on our Facebook Break the Travel Barrier page.

Breakthetravelbarrier.com is an extension of this book, with up-to-date travel directories, the best and latest deals, and additional tips, tricks, and stories. You will find a chat forum where you can connect with a worldwide network of like-minded travel bugs, share your stories, learn from others, and rejoice in our collective success. When you find yourself living that magical moment abroad, drop us a line to tell us how it feels! If you started this journey as a skeptic, congratulations for taking this journey anyway! Please join us in the forum, and share how this book helped you and whether you are traveling more, staying longer, or spending less.

Acknowledgements

To start, I'd like to acknowledge two people who are no longer amongst us, who played an instrumental role in this book. Robbie McHugh inspired me to share my stories in these pages, and Pierre-Louis Bertamini generously invited me into his home and offered me a helping hand. My memories of our time together will live on.

I want to extend my thanks and appreciation to everyone in my life, for their encouragement, enthusiasm, and understanding of the time demands required to embark on a journey to research and write a book.

If there is such a thing as divine intervention, I believe that is what brought me to the following people, as you would not be holding this book if it were not for their guidance, training, and support. Notably, my editors, Debra Englander, who is the only person to have seen this book in its rawest form, and David Yeager, who got it to the finish line. Thank you both for your time, devotion, and patience, as we transformed my garbled text into a book that I am proud to share with enthusiastic travelers.

Geoffrey Berwind opened my eyes to the power of storytelling and helped me put my experiences onto paper. I am grateful for the guidance and critique offered by Martha Bullen. Her coaching helped me steer clear of many pitfalls that trip up first-time authors. "Sound bites" would not be part of my regular vocabulary nor would they be sprinkled through this book, if it were not for Danette Kubanda. Thank you for also being there on a moment's notice, when I received my first invitation for my first media appearance.

My college friend Brett Fitzpatrick and his team at Red Door Media designed a book cover, website, and logo that exceeded all my expectations. You might not have heard about this book, had it not been for Bob Taylor (radio coach), Carl Bussler (video editor), and Brian Edmondson (internet marketing coach), who helped me bring my message to you.

Finally, I offer my sincere thanks and gratitude to Steve Harrison and Jack Canfield, who were with me every step of the way, through the Bestseller Blueprint program they offer to authors. Their Quantum Leap systems are the secrets to my success, and their influence and impact on the world are farther reaching than can ever be measured.

You are all world-class. It's my sincere hope that this book makes you all proud.

About the Author

Russell Hannon is an Ultra-Economical Travel Expert with Break the Travel Barrier and the author of Stop Dreaming ... Start Traveling. He has been featured in dozens of media segments, including national broadcasts such as America Tonight, and is a speaker on economical travel.

Russell is a passionate traveler at heart who thrives on minimizing the cost of travel without compromising. Once, feeling unable to afford to travel, Russell leveraged his lean management expertise to travel significantly more on the same budget, while saving time planning, and without compromising lifestyle. He has since taken more than a dozen free trips and visited some of the world's most expensive cities, for his at-home cost of living and sometimes less.

APPENDIX A – Travel Suitcase

FREE CARS

Drive Cars for People Relocating

U.S.: autodriveaway.com
Canada: hittheroad.ca

Inexpensive Rentals

autoslash.com is an online car rental booking website that continues looking for lower fares, even after you book, and rebooks you anytime it finds a lower fare for an identical itinerary.

FREE STAYS

Travel Hospitality

couchsurfing.com

globalfreeloaders.com

hospitalityclub.org

homestaybooking.com

homestayclub.com

homestayfinder.com

servas.org

wimdu.com – also offers private rentals

worldwidehomestay.com

Home Swapping

homeexchange.com: Featured in the movie *The Holiday*

homeforswap.com

thevacationexchange.com

Housesitting

caretaker.org

housecarers.com

housesit.org

housesitmatch.com (Australia and the U.K.)

luxuryhousesitting.com

mindmyhouse.com

trustedhousesitters.com

Group Travel Operators

Contact these travel operators and ask how many people you need to sign up at their going rate to get a free trip. This is a great option for college students who can put posters throughout the campus to recruit fellow students for a spring break getaway.

gadventures.com

go-today.com

freeandeasytraveler.com

Intrepid Travel

Repair hiking trails for room and board

americanhiking.org

continentaldividetrail.org

World Wide Organic Farming

wwoof.org

wwoofinternational.org

More Voluntour Opportunities for Free Accommodations

caretaker.org

globalvolunteers.org

helpx.net

idealist.org

podvolunteer.org

rotary.org

unitedplanet.org

volunteervacations.com

INEXPENSIVE ACCOMMODATIONS

Sorted from Least-to-Most Expensive

National Campground Directories

Australia: camping.com.au

Canada: camping-canada.com

Europe:

campingcheque.com: Access over 640 campsites in 29 countries for as little as 16 Euros a night.

campingeurope.com

eurocampings.co.uk

europe-camping-holiday.com

camping.info

New Zealand: tourism.net.nz

U.S. & Canada: uscampgrounds.info

Attend Timeshare Presentations for Discounted, Fully Furnished Accommodation

intervalworld.com

clubintrawest.com

diamondresorts.com

hiltongrandvacations.com

hyattresidenceclub.com

orangelake.com

rci.com

shellvacationsclub.com

westgateresorts.com

wyndhamvacationresorts.com

Shared Accommodations

airbnb.com

homeaway.com

stayrentals.com

transitionsabroad.com

wimdu.com

Vacation Rentals

vrbo.com (Vacation Rentals by Owner)

Hostels

hostelbookers.com

hostelworld.com

Bed & Breakfasts

bedandbreakfast.com

bedandbreakfastworld.com

Hotels

backbid.com: Post your booking and competing hotels will try to sway you with better offers.

eurocheapo.com: Cheap hotels in Europe.

hotels.com: Get one free night for every 10 bookings.

travelpony.com: Often offers better prices than other websites in dozens of cities.

trivago.com: Search more than 650,000 hotels, from more than 150 websites.

Hotel Price Drop Refunds

tingo.com: If prices drop after you book, tingo automatically refunds the difference

Daytime Stays

dayguest.com: Offers discounts for daytime-only stays.

Last Minute Hotels

hoteltonight.com

lastminute.com

room77.com

For the Distinguished Traveler

wantmegetme.com: Offers upgrades, special treatment, and free Wi-Fi at five-star hotels.

International Cruise Line Directory

routesinternational.com

CHEAP FLIGHTS

Get Real-Time Price Drop Notifications

farecomparc.com

yapta.com

Round the World Tickets

airtreks.com: Specializes in complex multi-stop international journeys.

Airline Alliances

oneworld.com

skyteam.com

staralliance.com

Flight Specific Search Engines

airfairewatchdog.com

flightnetwork.com

google.com/flights

pintrips.com

selloffvacations.com (Canada)

theflightdeal.com

whichbudget.com

ALL-IN-ONE SEARCH ENGINES

airgorilla.com

baseops.net/marketplace: Discounts for U.S. military.

cheaptickets.com

expedia.com

hotwire.com

kayak.com

lowfares.com

momondo.com

monograms.com

orbitz.com

priceline.com

shermanstravel.com

slickdeals.net

vayama.com

venere.com

travelocity.com

travelzoo.com

tripadvisor.com

Last Minute Travel Deals

lastminute.com

lastminutetravel.com

travelocity.com

travelzoo.com

tripadvisor.com

Canada Specific

airtransat.com

escapes.ca

itravel2000.com

selloffvacations.com

sunwing.ca

Group Travel Operators

gadventures.com

go-today.com

freeandeasytraveler.com

Intrepid Travel

FUND YOUR TRAVELS

Crowd Funding

fundanything.com

fundly.com

fundrazr.com

gofundme.com

gogetfunding.com

peerbackers.com

Watch my video on how run successful travel fundraisers online at: https://www.youtube.com/watch?v=m-ske_W7-HA

Track the Biggest and Best Travel Rewards Promotions

cardsfortravel.com

flyertalk.com

milepoint.com

rewardscanada.ca

rocketmiles.com

pointshound.com

boardingarea.com

thepointsguy.com

travelhacking.org

Browse the Best Rewards Credit Cards

cardsfortravel.com

FIND A JOB ABROAD

Great Resources to Get Started

goabroad.com

transitionsabroad.com

International Employment Agencies

ccusa.com

theworkingholidayclub.com

International Jobs

americanhiking.org: Repair hiking trails. Volunteer programs also offered.

care.com: Nanny jobs, housekeeping, and pet sitting.

goabroad.com

gooverseas.com: Teach English, intern, study, volunteer.

transitionsabroad.com: For young Americans seeking work, study, and accommodations abroad.

unitedplanet.org: For mid-career professionals taking career breaks to travel.

workpermit.com: Country-by-country work permit information.

Internships

gapyear.com: The British-based site for international internships.

Teach English Abroad

languagecourse.net: Shows you how to get TESOL or TEFL certified.

gooverseas.com: Opportunities to teach English abroad.

Cruise Ship Jobs

routesinternational.com

carnival.com

celebrity.com

costacruise.com

hollandamerica.com

ncl.com

princess.com

royalcaribbean.com

How to Get into the Cruise Line Industry

allcruisejobs.com

cruiselinejobs.com

STUDENT TRAVEL

International Student Discount Cards

isic.org: For full-time students of any age.

statravel.com

travelcuts.com

Student Travel Websites

itravelosophy.com: International student travel operator.

letsgo.com: Created by students for students.

studentuniverse.com: Offers group trips and free support to youth between 18 and 25 years of age.

rotary.org

Subsidized Student Travel Experiences

Bestdelegate.com: Participate in mock UN sessions, to understand how the UN works and develop diplomatic and negotiation skills. Sessions take place all over the U.S., including the actual UN hall in New York!

APPENDIX B

Dream Travel Plan – Travel Planning Form

The first step most people take in planning their trip is often the wrong one. For the most part, they want to go to the same places, at the same times, as everyone else and overlook equally fulfilling opportunities that can cost a lot less.

What You Need To Know: You'll never find the best price at the moment you suddenly decide you want to go somewhere.

Slash the Cost of Your Next Trip

There is no one place on earth you have to see so badly today that no other place can compensate. So, take this approach to eventually visit all the places you want to see at a fraction of the cost:

1. Make your bucket list. List the top 10 destinations you want to visit.

If You Like	I Suggest
Spectacular natural scenery	South Africa
Geographical extremes in close proximity	Tanzania
Beaches	Thailand, Philippines, Vietnam
Mega cities	Mumbai, Manila

2. Define your top travel interests (what you want to get out of your travels). Common examples include: family vacation, visit friends, girl's getaway, let loose, decompress, etc. …

3. Tag the appropriate interests to each destination

4. For each destination, note how you will get there and where you will stay

5. Prioritize your bucket list from least to most expensive, then in accordance with this scale:

All Other Things Being Equal:				
	1	Short Window of Opportunity		Available Anytime
	2	Truly Free Accommodations		Free Accommodations by redeeming non-financial means
Prioritize	3	Options you can fund with non-financial means	**OVER**	Options requiring you to pay out of pocket
	4	Accommodations with kitchens		Accommodations requiring you to eat out every meal
	5	Free Accommodations		Free Transportation
*If two destinations are tied on your short list, go with your favorite option				

*If two destinations are tied on your short list, prioritize your favorite.

Once you're done, your short list will look like this:

Destination	Tag 1	Tag 2	Accommodations	Transportation	Priority Number
1. San Francisco	Visit Friend	–	Free – Adam's place	Car – 5 hour drive	1 (Next Trip)
2. Melbourne	Winter	Escape	Hotel – rewards points	Flight rewards points	2
3. Geneva	Explore	Adventure	Camping	$1,100 (Fly, car rental)	3

Dream Travel Planning Form

Destination	Tag 1	Tag 2	Accommodations	Transportation	Priority

1. ____________________
2. ____________________
3. ____________________
4. ____________________
5. ____________________
6. ____________________
7. ____________________
8. ____________________
9. ____________________
10. ____________________

On-Hold

Travel Advisory In-Effect: ____________________

Potential Business Trip: ____________________

APPENDIX C

Travel Writing Sales Solicitation Template

Attention: Content Director/Manager Name
From: Your name – Travel Writer
Your Contact Information
Your Website

Dear _______,

You are certainly interested in unique literary content that can captivate your audience. As a long time reader of ______ and an established travel writer who has published _______, I see an opportunity to engage your audience with an article on the subject of _______. Knowing they have an interest in ______, they would certainly be fascinated to learn about _______.

I will be writing an article on this topic during an upcoming trip to _______, taking place from ____ to _____. I would first like to speak with you to get a better understanding of your guidelines and to answer any questions you may have.

You are welcome to review my writing portfolio at _____ and to contact me through the information provided below. Having been a long time reader of your publication, I am looking forward to speaking with you.

Cordially,
Name
Contact Information
Website Address
Link to Social Media Feeds

References

[1]Paul Morrow, (2010). First Around the World, retrieved January 12 2013.

[2]Ford, H. & Crowther, S. (1922). My Life and Work. Garden City, New York, USA: Garden City Publishing Company Inc.

[3]Donna Fuscaldo, Bankrate.com (2012), House swapping a vacation stay. Retrieved August 28, 2013.
Sara Tetreault (2012), Frugal can be stylish, fancy and fun, I'm here to show you how. Retrieved August 28, 2013.

[4]NBC News Travel, Travelkit segment (2012), Hotels on track to take in nearly 2 billion in surcharges, retrieved on April 4, 2013.

[5]Helium.com, Robert Schoenburg. An RR Donnelley company (2008), No Frill Airlines. Content License issued to Break the Travel Barrier. January, 16, 2014.

[6]Grit & Glamour (2011), Tax Deductions and Blogging—What You Need to Know, retrieved January 3 2014.
Gordon Burgett (2013), What do you do first to deduct your travel writing trips? retrieved January 3, 2014.

[7]The Associated Press, Josef Federman (2013), Israeli start up seeks to end roaming charges for global travellers, retrieved on January 24, 2014.

CPSIA information can be obtained at www.ICGtesting.com
Printed in the USA
LVOW08s1250180416

484132LV00002B/146/P